"Denise Allen knows the love of God. Through deep and wonderful encounters with Holy Spirit, she writes from a heart overflowing. *The Window Box Series, Pathways to Peace* will touch your soul. Full of insights into God's heart and the ways He speaks to us, you will be encouraged as you turn each page. Get ready for the indescribable love of your Father to wash over you. I love this book!"

—Brian Simmons,
The Passion Translation Project

"Denise writes with sensitivity and understanding, coming from a lifetime of walking with God. Her words inspire deep reflection and bring healing of the wounds of life. She writes with vulnerability about the difficult experiences in her own life and brings God's message of transformation."

—Bruce Pajot,
M.Div., M.A. LPC, LMHC

"Denise takes you on a spiritual and emotional healing journey, told through the pages of her own life in this one of a kind devotional. Personal and beautifully raw life lessons that guide you into victories in some of life's most difficult situations and circumstances. Denise is a wife, a mom, a daughter, a sister, and a friend. For as long as I've known her, she has had a heart to empower women, to encourage them in their struggles, and to lead them into a victorious lifestyle. So I wholeheartedly recommend *The Window Box Series, Pathways to Peace* for anyone, man or woman, who needs encouragement, who needs help, and who needs to know that God is on their side."

—Colette Trazinski,
Pastor/Missionary

PATHWAYS TO PEACE

THE WINDOW BOX SERIES

DENISE ALLEN

Copyright © 2020 by Denise Allen

All rights reserved.

No part of this book may be reproduced in any form or by any electronic or mechanical means, including information storage and retrieval systems, without written permission from the author, except for the use of brief quotations in a book review.

Hardcover: ISBN 978-1-953314-00-0

Paperback: ISBN 978-1-953314-01-7

Library of Congress Control Number: 2020915446

Photographs by Denise Allen

Published by:

    Messenger Books
    1629 Brookhollow Dr.
    Lindale, TX 75771
    Messengerbooks.com

Scriptures marked KJV are taken from the KING JAMES VERSION (KJV): KING JAMES VERSION, public domain.

Scriptures marked ASV are taken from the American Standard Version (ASV): American Standard Version, public domain

Scriptures marked TPT are taken from THE PASSION TRANSLATION (TPT): Scripture taken from THE PASSION TRANSLATION®. Copyright© 2017 by Passion and Fire Ministries, Inc. Used by permission. All rights reserved. ThePassionTranslation.com.

To my parents:

*My Dad, Charles, for passing on to me the love of words and writing.
My Mom, Dolores, for teaching me the gift of compassion.*

To my husband:

Jesse, the love of my life.

To my children:

Jay, Dan and Julia, the treasures of my life.

To Jesus,

the Keeper of my soul.

And to all my dear friends at the Window Box.

CONTENTS

Introduction	ix
1. Renovation	1
Journal	5
2. Changes	6
Journal	11
3. These Hands	12
Journal	16
4. The Prisoner	17
Journal	22
5. Hope	23
Journal	27
6. The Gift of Motherhood	28
Journal	33
7. The Two Dollar Bill Man, Signs, and Wonders	34
Journal	39
8. Perseverance	40
Journal	45
9. Let Grace Sing	46
Journal	51
10. Betrayal	52
Journal	59
11. Guilt	60
Journal	65
12. Heavenly Encounters	66
Journal	71
13. Where the Homeless Live	72
Journal	79
14. Beauty in the Desert	80
Journal	85
15. The Artist	86
Journal	91
16. A Father	92

Journal	97
17. The Power of Self-Acceptance	98
Journal	103
18. The Day the World Stopped	104
Journal	109
19. Melody	110
Journal	115
20. Sisterhood	116
Journal	121
21. The Treasure	122
Journal	127
22. The Day I Lost My Best Friend	128
Journal	133
23. Letting Go	134
Journal	137
24. Antennas	138
Journal	143
25. The Bully & Arbor Day	144
Journal	149
26. The Riptides of Life	150
Journal	155
27. No Fear	156
Journal	161
28. "Mom, Breathe! I'm OKAY!"	162
Journal	167
29. The Sunflower	168
Journal	171
30. Two Words	172
Journal	177
31. Denise's Window Box	178
Journal	183
Epilogue	184
About the Author	187

A Note from the Author

~

Dear Reader,

In my book, *Pathways to Peace*, there are 31 reflective stories. Each story is a personal narrative from my life to reflect on certain lessons learned with an impartation of inner healing and forgiveness.

I've included photos from my personal collection to set the mood for each story to reflect upon. Also included is a prayer at the end of each story to provide peace, hope and comfort.

A space for journaling your own thoughts and prayers is provided for the reader after each story. It is my hope that these stories and prayers give you the inspiration to follow through on your own pathway to peace.

In *Pathways to Peace,* I share many of my life moments where the road often got messy and unclear. I felt lost at times. It was during these times, somewhere down the road, where I found myself safe by reflecting on my inner strength, God and prayer.

I hope that you, also, on your journey, will know these *Pathways to Peace*.

Join me in the journey.

Sincerely yours,
Denise

1

RENOVATION

I had been anticipating my sun porch renovation for a long time. I longed for tropical green plants, pretty colored pillows on my white wicker couch and aqua blue walls with a crisp white ceiling. Instead, I had been looking at dull white walls with worn wood and a ceiling in dire need of paint and repair. It had become a storage room of sorts, with tools, paint cans, bikes and building supplies. The room was dark and forlorn, looking somewhat hopeless. However, in my heart, I kept the vision of a lovely sun porch where I could have my morning coffee with the bright sunshine smiling at me and plants proudly displaying their colors.

In the meantime, I made cute little pillows and painted word signs that read, "Love," "Live" and "Faith." I repainted the furniture with colors true to my heart, knowing one day I would have a room where I could read my favorite books, write reflective thoughts and pray special prayers, all the while, listening to nice music I enjoyed.

The day finally arrived for the long awaited renovation. There is much involved in a renovation, depending on what needs to be reconstructed and repaired. In this case, the first thing needed was removing all of the clutter. It was everywhere, from old paint cans to damaged tools, bikes and numerous totes. Once all the clutter was clear, cleaning was necessary to rid the room of all dust and dirt. Then the walls, ceilings, floor and baseboards needed to be repaired. Some of the wood was weak and split, and other pieces needed to be replaced.

Finally, the paint could be poured in all the pretty colors chosen. There were aqua blues and crisp whites with touches of pastel greens on the painted furniture pieces. Then, I lovingly placed the green plants in their sunny spots and fluffed the pretty pillows in position on the newly painted wicker couch. The renovation was complete. It was a completely different atmosphere with no clutter or broken, worn-out pieces. It was crisp and clean, full of bright light, giving way to new life as I had envisioned.

As I sat in my newly transformed, renovated sun porch room that first sunny morning, drinking my hot coffee, I reflected on my faith. At times, it too, needed renovation. There were times it was worn out, broken and weak, cluttered with worries and burdens, needing repair and restoration. When our faith is tried and tested, it often stretches us to the point where we may feel broken and weak, and there are times when it is broken and weak. This is when we are in need of some reconstruction and renovation. This is when we need to ask God for more faith and the tools we need to repair and restore our faith.

I have found that when we ask God for faith and restoration, He is faithful to do just that. He is the true renovator making all things new, restoring the broken and weary places of our heart and faith. All we need to do is ask. As we give our cluttered and damaged places to Him, He is ready and able to reconstruct and repair. As we trust God and ask for more faith during the needed times of renovation in our life, He is faithful to lead and guide us to a brighter, safe and happy resting place.

> *Trust in the Lord completely, and do not rely on your own opinions. With all your heart rely on Him to guide you, and He will lead you in every decision you make.*
>
> —Proverbs 3:5, TPT

During these times of needing more faith in my life, when I felt broken and weak, in need of repair, I found myself asking God for more faith to believe, to trust, and to help me along life's cluttered way. I have found that He has proven to be gracious, rich in mercy and faithful to renovate those places in my heart and soul.

Dear Lord,

Thank You that You understand when we are in need of some renovation and repair. Thank You that You are faithful to do just that with Your loving kindness. I give You these tired and broken places in my faith and ask You for more faith to believe and trust again.

4 | PATHWAYS TO PEACE

Thank You for Your faithfulness to me in renovating these places.

In Jesus' name, I pray.

Amen.

> *Now, if anyone is enfolded into Christ, he has become an entirely **new creation**. All that is related to the old order has vanished. Behold, everything is fresh and **new**.*

—2 Corinthians 5:17, TPT
(emphasis added)

JOURNAL — One

<u>Your Personal Journal:</u>

There are times in our life when we are in need of some reconstruction and renovation to lead us to a place of peace. God is there to help us during these times.

Are there areas in your life that need some reconstruction? Let God help.

_____

_____

_____

_____

_____

_____

_____

_____

<u>Your Personal Prayer:</u>

_____

_____

_____

_____

_____

2

CHANGES

I sat there on my living floor looking at the echoes of a now empty room. Leaving my home of 30 years with only one suitcase in tow, knowing it was time to move on. The time for change had come to its reckoning and I was ready - ready or not. For months I went through belongings, such as my furnishings, collectibles, Christmas decor and even my indoor plants, which I considered my babies, categorizing them as what to keep, what to give away, or what to sell.

Changes | 7

It was a long, tiresome, sometimes grueling process of what I would let go of and what I wanted to keep. It took hours upon hours of work and organization, and totes upon totes! Yet that was just the physical part of it.

I had made moves before in my life. At age 19, I moved away from the town I grew up in to a state a few thousand miles away, which was a totally different climate and people. When I was 21, I moved from there. Then I found myself two years later, at the age of 23, moving once again. Drastic relocations happened several more times in my life as well! So, what was so different about this move?

Well, after several of these moves in my earlier years as a young adult, I came full circle and landed in the hometown I grew up in. I made a little family with my husband, and we lived there for the past 30 years. I knew every street, every shopping center, and every shortcut to get somewhere. I had a close knit community of friends and relationships. It was comfortable and familiar. Boring at times, but at least I knew my comings and goings without any guess work.

There was no denying it, transition was in our midst. My husband would soon be retiring and my daughter would soon be graduating high school, seeking out colleges. The rumblings of change were beginning to breathe upon us. It felt scary, exciting, confusing, fun and questionable.

Still, we couldn't deny that change was speaking to us. Change can be played out like a tug of war. You want it, but you don't. You need it, but are afraid of it. You sense it, but deny it. Go with it a little bit, then hold back. It's a funny thing in that it teases us with, "yes, no, yes no. Go, stay. Go, stay. Let go, but hold on." It is like the yellow blinking traffic light; stop, proceed... but with caution.

8 | PATHWAYS TO PEACE

I don't know about you, but I don't like caution, blinking, or warning lights in my life. I like the red stop, or the green go, with no fear in between. With change comes the what-ifs, the questions and not knowing everything like the back of your hand. It's exciting to think about, but creating it is actually a scary concept. This is completely normal because we like safe, comfortable and stable routines. We may get bored with them at times, but all in all, we feel safe and comfortable with them. Change is just that, change. It can be messy, ugly and frightening because it is the unknown.

So, there I was in my living room, knowing, but not knowing. My suitcase was packed, but my emotions were running a gamut. I was excited, anticipatory, somewhat fearful and somewhat mournful. I was fearful when I thought about all the what-ifs talking to me, and mournful of all the things and people I was leaving behind.

"It'll be Okay," I told myself. "I'm ready," I said to my heart and soul.

I walked to the window and looked at my flower gardens for one last time. The sunflowers stood tall and smiled as they faced the sun, the daisies sat pretty with such happiness and the green grass swayed with the breeze. They were all so beautiful, leaving their own valuable fragrance in the season that they were in.

So many times I have gathered them to make a lovely bouquet to bring into the house and enjoy their beauty and fragrance. Summer is the season where they thrive and blossom, giving off their loveliest fragrance and bloom. Fall is when I cut them back, and winter is when they are dormant. Each season holds a significant change for them. One cannot go without the other. Each season of change holds its purpose and value.

Changes | 9

So it was with us. It was time for my family and I to move on. To grow. To let go. To become. A future, destiny, and purpose awaits us. We had to follow the change in order to grow and become all that we were meant to be. As a tear trickled down my cheek, I embraced the mourning of letting go, moving on and the new season of change that laid before me.

This new season of change brought me from my suburban home in Connecticut, to a smaller home in Florida near the water. I am currently loving my new little home; decorating it with beachy themes of lighter colors and simple art and crafts that I enjoy making. My New England roots, with all its charm and quaintness, remain in my heart, and the newness of palm trees, gulf waters and bright sunshine have birthed new beginnings in me.

The seasons of change bring new awareness to our lives with new opportunities and blessings. Seasons of change are the cycles of life. God is faithful to lead and guide us through each one. Change has moved me to a place of writing this book.

So we are convinced that every detail of our lives is continually woven together to fit into God's perfect plan of bringing good into our lives, for we are his lovers who have been called to fulfill his designed purpose.

—Romans 8:28, TPT

Dear Lord,

Thank You for giving us the grace to move on. Thank You for the courage and wisdom needed to make changes. We trust You for the

10 | PATHWAYS TO PEACE

changes in the seasons of our life. You are faithful and loving, and You make everything beautiful in your time.

Amen.

JOURNAL — Two

<u>Your Personal Journal:</u>

When was a time when you needed a new beginning?

How did you find peace during your changing seasons?

_____

_____

_____

_____

_____

_____

_____

_____

_____

_____

<u>Your Personal Prayer:</u>

_____

_____

_____

_____

3
THESE HANDS

*H*ands tell many stories. Young hands. Old hands. A newborn baby's hands. Each set of hands tells a different story of past, present and future. These hands are of three generations—my mom, my daughters and mine. I have learned so much from these hands.

My mom's hands have caressed me with love in times of sickness and distress, cooking me chicken soup when I was ill and stroking my hair when I needed comfort. These same hands taught me to work hard as I watched her, as a working woman, getting ready for work each day then coming home to prepare supper each night. They have taught me to pray hard, love hard and embrace much.

Her lovely hands taught me to give and give some more. I saw her deep love for family and friends as she wrote out "Thinking of You" cards and never missed a beat sending off birthday cards to loved ones. It was those creative hands that washed, braided, combed and curled my hair, making me feel beautiful and lovely as a little girl. Her beautiful hands would cup my face and tell me how much I was loved.

Those hands would hold my chin up and in wisdom tell me to always be true to myself. Those hands were so gentle and strong at the same time. Oh, how I miss those hands. Those beautiful hands taught me courage, perseverance, strength and dignity. Those hands showed me gentleness, kindness and love. Such a legacy she left me in the gift of her hands.

I will always remember the day my daughter was born as I held her tender, soft, tiny, little beautiful hand. Her new life squeezed into mine with her precious and strong grip. As her Mom, my heart asked, "What will these precious hands do? What will they achieve? What will they conquer? How can I lead and guide them? So precious and special they are." So, I carefully and tenderly took her hand, as my mother did mine, to lead and guide and teach as the best I knew how.

I held her hand as I walked her to school. I guided her little hand as I taught her to use a fork and spoon. I grasped her hand as we crossed the street and taught her to go up and down stairs. I would stroke her hair at times to comfort her and make her chicken soup when she wasn't feeling well. I would cup her

14 | PATHWAYS TO PEACE

sweet little face in my hands and tell her how very much I loved her and to always be true to herself. I would hold my daughter's hands to teach her, guide her and love her as my Mom had done for me. At night, we would join our hands together to say our bedtime prayers.

Now, my daughter is teaching me—guiding and loving me with her tender, precious and strong hands. After having an accident and breaking my shoulder, she helps me brush my hair and makes me chicken soup. She holds my hand up and down the stairs. Her loving hands are helping me. Oh, those hands. They have grown up, and now, they teach me: how to use the newest iPhone, apply the latest makeup tips, and how to give and receive. There is life in these hands. They have stories to tell.

These hands of courage, strength, dignity, gentleness and strength—they hold a treasure of history of past, present and future. They impart destiny, hope, dreams and faith.

These hands of younger and older have helped guide, mold and shape me, teaching me all that I need to be. How lovely they are to me, and how forever thankful I will be.

I will hold these hands forever.

> *There's no doubt about it; God holds our lives safely in his hands. He's the one who keeps us faithfully following him.*

> —*Psalm 66:9, TPT*

Dear Father,

Thank You for these hands in my life. They are Your hands extended to me through the gift of love. They have taught me how to pray, how to love, how to give. Thank You for Your gift of life. Thank You for Your blessings to me.

Amen

JOURNAL — Three

Your Personal Journal:

Mothers and daughters are some of the most treasured relationships in life.

What have you learned in these relationships?

What are some of your most treasured moments?

_____

_____

_____

_____

_____

_____

_____

_____

Your Personal Prayer:

_____

_____

_____

_____

_____

4

THE PRISONER

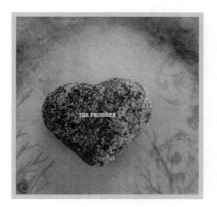

*A*s I walked down the cold, eerie corridor, I was met by guards who looked at me suspiciously, asking for my purse, ID and any other personal belongings I was carrying. I then walked through another security system, being frisked by a woman officer, making sure nothing was hidden under my clothing. We then were escorted down a dark, dingy hallway where locked, steel doors were opened for us. There, waiting for our arrival, was an audience of women prisoners.

18 | PATHWAYS TO PEACE

I was with a group of a dozen people who did outreach to women's prisons. This was my first encounter, and I was nervous. Not knowing what to expect, I could see the women in their orange jumpsuits nervously chattering. Some were even wringing their hands and also, like me, did not know what to expect. Perhaps some were there just to get away from their cells and "roommates."

Our group was there to play music, sing, pray and talk with them. During the week, I had been contemplating what to say and what to sing, and even tried talking myself out of going. However, I knew I had to listen to my innermost voice that told me to go and offer hope.

As I considered for several days what to share with these women prisoners, I was reminded of a childhood memory. When I was a little girl and had feelings of being distraught, alone or finding myself needing comfort, I would go to a neighbor's swing set across from my yard. There I would sit in the swing, look up into the sky, listen to the birds around me singing and I would begin to swing effortlessly and easily.

I would sing a song I learned in Sunday school: "Jesus loves me this I know, for the Bible tells me so. Little ones to Him belong. We are weak, but He is strong. Yes, Jesus loves me. Yes, Jesus loves me. Yes, Jesus loves me. The Bible tells me so." No matter how many times I sang that song, swinging in that swing set, it brought great comfort and joy to me. I remember I would swing higher and higher as the joy welled up inside of me. Sometimes I would swing slowly, almost caressing my soul as I felt the comfort envelope me.

I knew I was supposed to sing this to these women. "How simplistic," I thought. "They are not children, but women in prison." Hard, angry, tough women! Surely, there is something else I can read or talk about. However, the impression

The Prisoner | 19

to sing this simple song to them only grew stronger within me.

So, here I was. It was my turn to get up in front of them and introduce myself. As I looked out over the crowd, I saw many that weren't paying attention. I saw others slouched in their seats, looking bored and forlorn. There were angry faces, sad faces and empty faces. I began to share the story of the days I sat on the swing in my neighbor's yard.

Some snickered and laughed, others had no expression. Then, I began to sing, "Jesus loves you this I know, for the Bible tells me so. Little ones to Him belong. We are weak, but He is strong." I sang it again and again.

Three times I sang it. At first, many were laughing to one another quietly. They began squirming in their seats kind of uncomfortably, and then, I began to see tears streaming down some of their faces. The laughter turned into quietness. Some had their faces in their hands. Others were wiping tears away from their hardened faces.

When I finished, I simply said, "Jesus loves you so much."

When I went to sit back down in my seat, I decided instead to sit next to several of the women in orange. It was then that they began to ask me to pray for them. They told me their stories. They told me how they missed their children, husbands and parents. They told me how angry they were, how sorry they were and how lonely and scared they were. They cried with me, and I cried with them.

I realized that day, in a cold, dreary prison, with angry, sad, and bitter women in orange, a simple message can help heal a broken heart. I also realized that love drives out fear. I think they were just as afraid of me as I was of them, but love made a way for us to connect.

Even though I was not a prisoner living in that prison, there were times in my life where I felt angry, lonely, bitter, forsaken and even betrayed. There were times as a little girl where I went to that swing set to hear the birds sing, and I would sing my song of comfort.

> *"Jesus loves me this I know,*
> *for the Bible tells me so...*
> *Yes, Jesus loves me."*

We all have moments in our lives where we feel imprisoned. When we feel lonely, rejected, scared and are needing comfort, we need love to set us free. I discovered that day in that prison, where love seemed so far away, that it was right there in front of me. I just had to offer it. Despite my fears and judgments, I was called upon to love those women right where they were.

God's love is like that. It breaks the chains that want to hold us down and hold us back. It breaks the barriers of judgment and fear. I have learned, and I am still learning, that God's love makes all the difference to set the captives free.

> *If therefore the Son shall make you free, ye shall be free indeed.*
>
> —John 8:36, ASV

Dear Lord,

Thank You for Your love that is incredibly patient and kind: a love that forgives and heals, a love that never gives up. Your love drives

The Prisoner | 21

away fear and is a safe place of shelter. Heal us and free us to love ourselves and love others as You have loved us. Thank You for such a great love.

Amen.

JOURNAL — Four

Your Personal Journal:

We demonstrate God's love by giving it unconditionally. As we do, our fear diminishes and God's love is released.

What does God's love mean to you?

_____

_____

_____

_____

_____

_____

_____

_____

_____

_____

Your Personal Prayer:

_____

_____

_____

_____

_____

5
HOPE

The hospital hallways were long and held a medicinal odor, which always made me uncomfortable each time I visited my mother. Mom had become sick from her chemo treatments and landed several days in the hospital. I had come to visit her each night after my work day and the hallways were not getting any friendlier or more comfortable for me.

As I turned the corner to enter my mom's room, I found her sitting in a chair with her usual sweet smile greeting me. As weak as she was, she always had a smile and warm heart to greet me. Mom, so sweet, kind and loving, was now fighting the battle of her life. Still, she was ever so beautiful with her deep brown eyes, long, thick black hair and beautiful flawless skin.

It was her nature to put others first, so it was no surprise to me that she asked about my day, my children and my week, even though I knew she was weak and in pain. She then asked me if I would brush her hair, as she was just too weak to do so. Mom always had long, dark and thick hair. Her shiny, black, gorgeous hair really set her dark brown eyes off just beautifully. She was very captivating and lovely.

I reached for her hairbrush on her nightstand and began brushing the backside of her hair. With the first stroke came a few black strands of her lovely dark hair. With the second stroke, several more came, and by the third stroke, a few pieces came out. I wanted to gasp! I was not expecting this. Not yet! Not now! This was not supposed to happen so suddenly! No! I realized I kind of stopped talking, and Mom said, "How is my hair? Is it falling out?" I did not know what to say. I didn't want to lie, but I didn't want to tell the truth either.

I stood there behind her holding clumps of her gorgeous black shiny hair in my hand. I was trying to think how I could hide it from her. Maybe I could go to the bathroom and flush it down the toilet. I really did not want her to see it. I did not want to see it. It was painful and heart wrenching for me to see. As I clasped her beautiful black hair in my fist and made a dash for the bathroom, I simply said with tears in my eyes, "Oh, it's not too bad." I did not want her to see my tears or the fist full of hair in my hands.

Hope | 25

I realized then that I needed to give my mom hope. No matter how scared and frightened I was, I needed to give her hope. No matter how sad and desperate I felt, my Mom needed hope. It was her, now, that needed hope.

It had always been my mom that I went to when my heart and spirit were in need of hope.

During my lonely teenage years, where I felt alone and insecure, Mom would give me hope through her loving words of strength and courage. During my pregnancy, when I felt tired and fatigued, she was always there to offer help and encouragement.

Her voice of hope helped me to raise teens of my own.
Her voice of hope helped with financial struggles.
Her voice of hope always gave me courage.
Her voice of hope always gave me love.
Her voice of hope always gave me strength.
Her voice of hope was always there.

Here I was, needing hope at this very moment, seeing her weak and tired and losing her hair. Hope resonates that things will not always be this way. Hope is looking ahead and believing things will get better. This is what my mother always gave me as a daughter, as a woman and as a friend. As a child having nightmares, as a teen facing loneliness and depression, as a woman dealing with stress, my mom was a giver of hope.

When I came back from the bathroom, I feared what she would ask me next. "How bad was it? Did I lose a lot? It's falling out isn't it?"

Instead, she squeezed my hand. This was a message of hope. I knew that was hope speaking to me. I squeezed her hand back.

26 | PATHWAYS TO PEACE

We didn't have to say anything to each other, for hope had spoken.

Hope has many languages. It gives courage, sight and renewed vision. It has the ability to restore and heal. Hope brings life. Mom never cried about losing all her dark luscious hair, at least not to me. Perhaps she didn't want to tarnish my hope, seeing her cry.

Her hope made a difference in my life and that's what hope does. She has taught me to be a giver of hope to my children, husband, and friends, and to the world around me.

Now the God of hope fill you with all joy and peace in believing, that ye may abound in hope, in the power of the Holy Spirit.

—Romans 15:13, ASV

~

Dear Lord,

Let there be more of Your hope and light within me to give to others. You are the divine hope. May Your hope renew our strength and faith. Thank You for hope and the light and life it brings.

Amen.

JOURNAL — Five

<u>Your Personal Journal:</u>

Hope looks ahead and tells us that things will get better. Hope gives courage, strength and renewed vision. Hope leads us to peace.

What does hope mean to you?

_____

_____

_____

_____

_____

_____

_____

_____

_____

<u>Your Personal Prayer:</u>

_____

_____

_____

_____

_____

6

THE GIFT OF MOTHERHOOD

I was twenty three when I gave birth to my first child. I thought I had read every book on motherhood—from breastfeeding, to discipline, to teaching them motor skills. I soon learned it did not matter how many books one reads about motherhood, it can only prepare you for so much.

Each mother is different, and each child has different motherly needs—not to say the books and materials I obsessed over didn't help me, as it did to some degree. I realized though that I

The Gift of Motherhood | 29

had to learn on my own. Each child was a growing, learning experience.

I have three children: two sons and one daughter. Each one is different in their personality and expressions of personhood, and each one is an absolute delight. I count them as my treasures from heaven. For them I wanted to be the perfect mother, so I divulged myself in books, blogs and lectures on motherhood. I took notes and saved articles on motherhood. I listened to other moms' advice and grand wisdom on motherhood. I hoped I had all the answers to help guide me along the way to avoid mistakes and derailments on my part.

My daughter was colicky for what felt like a year and a day. It seemed like no matter what I did, nothing helped. I had to succumb to the fact that I was not a perfect mother.

There was the time my son, when he was nine years old, decided to jump on the trampoline with his roller blades on and ended up with a broken elbow. "Where was your mother when you did this?" the emergency room doctor asked. Again, I realized I was not the perfect mother.

It was the same thing when my eleven year old fell off a tree branch and broke his wrist. I think the doctor was ready to report me. A perfect mother I was not. The books did not prepare me for this.

What helped ease these moments, and when I felt absolutely perfect, was when they would hug and squeeze me at bedtime and tell me they loved me all the way to Mars. I knew I was the best Mom when they told me I was way cooler, nicer and prettier than all the other moms. To hear them say out of the blue, "I love you, Mom," affirmed to me I did something right after all.

I tried to learn so much to be the best mom possible by reading books and gleaning from all the latest material I could. It is such a gift to be a mother. I wanted to give the best guidance and be the best mentor I could be, while not being too strict, too easy, too silly or too firm. After all, it is one of the most monumental, if not the most significant jobs there is, at least to this mother.

You are changing hats all the time: from cook to taxi driver, psychologist, teacher, nurse, playmate, cheerleader, etcetera. The list goes on. I wouldn't trade it for the world. I have made mistakes, many of them along the way, as did my children. However, one of the most wonderful things about this is that my three children loved me along the way, and I loved them, always, no matter what.

An unconditional love is born between child and mother. It is a significant bond like no other, which is the great thing about being a mother. You give and receive. I will always remember their first smile at me, their first kiss to me and their first "I love you" to me. Even now, all grown up as adults, to see their smile, receive their hug and to hear "I love you, Mom" makes my heart sing and my spirit soar. To see their accomplishments and how they overcome the challenges and obstacles of life with courage and perseverance, not only gives me great joy, but it pushes me on to pursue my own dreams with courage and perseverance.

As a mother, I wanted to learn so much so I could be the perfect mother to my children, giving them all they needed. Yet, all the while, they were teaching me. I was learning from them how to love and how to give. I was learning how to be patient, kind and forgiving. I was learning how to trust. I was learning how to learn and not give up on myself, or them. I was learning the significance of the phrase, "there is no perfect." I was learning that the perfect is found in loving.

The Gift of Motherhood | 31

Each one of my children have different qualities I have learned from. I couldn't possibly have learned these qualities from any book or lecture. Their love has changed my life. Their smile has given me hope, and their personhood has helped develop mine.

This gift of motherhood has changed my life. It has taught me that love has no limits. It has been the greatest honor of my life. Love has been the most valuable thing I could have learned from three of the most valuable people in my life.

For where thy treasure is, there will thy heart be also.

—Matthew 6:21, ASV

Dear God,

Thank You for this gift of motherhood. Thank You for my three treasures. Continue to help me be the best mother I can possibly be. Keep Your guiding eyes on my children to lead them and guide them in Your truth and wisdom. Thank You for Your love in our lives.

Amen.

JOURNAL — Six

<u>Your Personal Journal:</u>

Motherhood has changed my life. It has been the most difficult challenge and my richest treasure. There are many different mothers: single mothers, divorced mothers, adoptive mothers; the list is endless. All are of great value and are assets.

What does motherhood mean to you?

What are some of your challenges in motherhood?

What are some of your accomplishments?

_____

_____

_____

_____

_____

_____

_____

<u>Your Personal Prayer:</u>

_____

_____

_____

_____

_____

7

THE TWO DOLLAR BILL MAN, SIGNS, AND WONDERS

It was a typical day at the restaurant during the noon, lunch-time hour. Waiters and waitresses were busily taking orders and making friendly chatter with their regulars. One regular was known as the "Two Dollar Bill Man."

The servers always contended with one another to see who could get to him first. He wasn't that demanding of a customer, but he knew what he wanted, how he wanted it and excellent

The Two Dollar Bill Man, Signs, and Wonders | 35

service was to be expected. He was friendly and courteous with a no-nonsense attitude. It should be served diligently and in a timely manner—with hot food, hot, and cold food, cold. Then he would reward accordingly, with a generous tip of two dollar bills.

He was respected and the servers would scurry over to him as fast and best they could. Then, when he finished eating and left his table, his white linen napkin would be neatly folded next to several two dollar bills. Each two dollar bill would have a distinct, black check mark or red dot in the corner. That was his trademark.

Each one of the servers saved their two dollar bills and would compete with each other as to who had the most. So there was always a contest amongst them of who could collect the most two dollar bills. This of course gave the "Two Dollar Bill Man" the best service and the waiters and waitresses a fun contest.

The Two Dollar Bill Man was often seen giving his grandkids, neighbors, grocery clerks, nieces and nephews two dollar bills on their birthdays or family gatherings. His face would light up with excitement and pleasure, not only in the giving, but also in watching the expressions of those receiving. He got a kick out of the responses.

Some asked if the two dollar bills were real. Others would ask where he got them. Some would hold them up to the light to see if there was a forgery of any kind, but most would enjoy the surprise of getting one and be giddy with excitement.

It is said the Two Dollar Bill Man would go to the bank every few weeks and exchange some twenties, or a hundred, for two dollar bills. These two dollar bills would be brand new and crisp. He would then take them home, line them across the table and mark each one with a black check mark or red dot in the corner of the bill.

I knew the Two Dollar Bill Man did these particular things because the Two Dollar Bill Man was my Dad. I would watch with glee when he would give them to my children or the neighborhood kids. He had a twinkle in his mischievous eye, waiting to see their reaction, which was always one of, "Oh! Awesome!"

I also was working at a restaurant during this time when the servers from another restaurant came in. They were talking about the two dollar tipper. I listened with a smile and twinkle in my eye. I told them I knew him, too.

They said excitedly, "You do?" I replied, "Yes! I sure do! That's my father." They couldn't believe it! They laughed excitedly and began telling me their stories of how they all competed with each other to wait on him when he would visit the restaurant and how they each began calling him the "Two Dollar Bill Man" or the "Two Dollar Tipper."

Well, my Dad passed away several weeks after this conversation. I took several weeks off my job to be home with my family. Upon returning to my job, my manager took me aside and asked if he could see me in his office.

I could not imagine what for, since my time away had been approved. When I entered his office, he handed me a white envelope. He told me that several people from the other restaurant had come in, and they had this white envelope for me. Since I was not there, they asked my manager if he would please give the envelope to me upon returning.

I left my manager's office with the white envelope in my hand then went to a quiet area in the restaurant and opened it. In it were several, brand new, crisp, two dollar bills, all marked with a black check mark in the corner. They had given me the two dollar bills my father had given them when he visited their restaurant.

As tears streamed down my cheeks, I felt heaven's love grab my heart with such joy and warmth. I could only look up and say, "Thank you, God, for this sign and wonder of Your great love towards me."

Many years went by, and the two dollar conversation would come up with family and friends, bringing back fond memories. It was a fun and loving legacy that my Dad left with friends and family, as well as acquaintances and strangers.

One day, as I was traveling several states away from home and feeling quite homesick, I needed to make a stop at a bank to get some change. The teller asked me if I would mind receiving some two dollar bills. With a big smile, I announced to her that I would love them. Getting back into my car, I looked at the two dollar bill, crisp and brand new. It was stamped in red with the words, "God loves you." My heart melted.

Once again, heaven was there, letting me know that I am loved, cared for and thought of. I looked up and said, "Thank you, God, for the Two Dollar Bill Man." I was smiling, and I have a feeling, He was smiling too.

> *O God, how extravagant is your cherishing love!*
>
> —Psalm 36:7, TPT

Dear God,

38 | PATHWAYS TO PEACE

Thank You that You speak to us in signs and wonders to remind us of Your great love towards us. How wonderful are Your ways in letting us know that nothing goes unnoticed with You. In big and wonderful ways, You let us know of Your great love for us.

Thank You, God.

Amen.

JOURNAL — Seven

<u>Your Personal Journal:</u>

What treasured memories do you have of someone special in your life?

Consider the ways God has reminded you of their love for you.

_____

_____

_____

_____

_____

_____

_____

_____

_____

<u>Your Personal Prayer:</u>

_____

_____

_____

_____

_____

8
PERSEVERANCE

Consider it pure joy, my brothers and sisters, whenever you face trials of many kinds, because you know that the testing of your faith produces perseverance. Let perseverance finish its work so that you may be mature and complete, not lacking anything.

—James 1:2-4, NIV

Perseverance | 41

*P*erseverance is hard work. I have not known it to be pure joy. In fact, I have known it to be quite the opposite. It has tested my strength, stamina, patience and endurance to my wits end! Perseverance is not a fun thing. It is difficult.

I enjoy riding my bike—leisurely riding that is. I am by no means a Lance Armstrong or competitive rider. I enjoy a simple ride, usually slow and easy, appreciating the scenery around me: flowers, blue skies and children playing.

One day during one of these leisurely rides, feeling fine under the sunshine, I had rounded the corner to turn into my driveway, when I somehow lost my balance. I crashed into our cement steps, landing with my shoulder hitting the corner of the step! The pain seared through my shoulder. As I thought I could get up, I quickly fell again, hard, onto the same area of my shoulder. The pain dominated my entire being, and I could not get up, much less move.

To make matters worse, my husband was not home. He had made a trip to the grocery store, and I lay there on the pavement, moaning and crying in terrible pain, wondering how long it would be before his arrival. I knew something was terribly wrong and wondered just how bad it was.

When my husband did arrive, which wasn't too much longer (although it felt like hours), he got me to the hospital, where I received the bad news that I broke my humerus bone in two places. The swelling had already started of course, which intensified the pain even more. I had never broken a bone before. I gave birth to three children naturally, but this pain was different. It hurt badly and would not go away. If you've ever had a bone break before, you know exactly what I'm talking about! I did not need surgery even though the breaks were significant.

However, I would be in a sling for weeks and need physical therapy for additional weeks.

Now, here is where the perseverance comes in. I slept on a recliner for 3 weeks, and when I finally did sleep in my bed, I had to sleep on my back. I am a side sleeper...and a tosser! This was not easy, so I missed a significant amount of sleep. I had to kind of roll out of bed, without daring to even slightly put any pressure or movement at all on my shoulder.

All my cooking was now one handed. Brushing my teeth, a simple task, was now difficult to finagle. I needed help getting dressed and showered. Simple tasks like brushing my hair, putting on my makeup and texting, suddenly became difficult.

Patience is a virtue they say! Oh, please!

Once I was healed enough to begin physical therapy, little did I realize that this, too, would be an act of my discipline and hard work. I had limited mobility and strength, along with the aches and pains of the still broken and damaged shoulder. Each session of therapy pushed me to do a "little bit" more and that "little bit" was exhausting. I never felt like it was enough to get it better and yet, that was all I was able to do at the time.

I had to persevere if it was going to get better and stronger again. I would also do the physical therapy exercises at home, even when I didn't feel like it. I was discouraged physically and emotionally. I didn't see much progress being made, and, oftentimes, I thought my shoulder would never be the same.

Perseverance often feels that way. It is hard work. It is a discipline of body, mind, soul and spirit. We often don't feel strong when we are persevering through something. As a matter of fact, we feel the opposite: tired, weary, weak, defeated. We feel like we will never reach our goal!

Perseverance | 43

However, as we persevere, a substance is being developed within us—a substance more valuable than gold. It is a lasting substance of stamina, strength and well-being.

Giving birth is a great example of perseverance. With my first-born, laboring for 7 hours, I well tasted the pains of perseverance. I chose natural childbirth and did not even take an aspirin or Tylenol. Anyone remember the Lamaze childbirth method? I thought I would do my breathing exercises while my husband would sweetly quote the scripture verses I had written down for him to recite as encouragement to me! Ummm, that didn't last too long, as the labor intensified. Ah yes, perseverance! It often comes with blood, sweat and tears. The pain intensified. The need to persevere intensified, but soon the birth arrived. A perfect, blue-eyed, beautiful son! Crying, shaking and yes, he had endured his own perseverance!

Perseverance has a plan. It may take us through valleys and hills, deep waters and fires. It is used to test us to see if we are going to jump over that hurdle, kick the obstacle out of the way and keep going, even if it's difficult. However, when perseverance has its perfect work, we are made better, stronger, and more durable. The substance within us is made more valuable. You are being made a better and healthier person, with a stronger character and well-being, not only for yourself, but for others.

During difficult times of perseverance, let us remember that even though our faith and endurance are being tested, we are being perfected. Our character is being developed and hope is being formed. Remember, this perseverance will yield its fruit in its season.

Keep pressing through! Keep going forward! There is a substance being formed, and it is gold.

44 | PATHWAYS TO PEACE

My fellow believers, when it seems as though you are facing nothing but difficulties see it as an invaluable opportunity to experience the greatest joy that you can!

—James 1:2, TPT

Dear Lord,

I surrender my weakness and my unwillingness to You. I need Your strength and Your stamina to see me through. Cause me to persevere, and equip me with what I need. I surrender to You and thank You for all that You are forming within me to make me better, to make me healthier in body, mind and spirit. For Your work is perfect, and You love me.

Amen.

JOURNAL — Eight

Your Personal Journal:

During seasons of perseverance, our character is being formed and shaped. As we keep pressing through and moving forward, we reap the benefits of our reward.

What can you focus on during times of perseverance?

What are some of the benefits and rewards of preserving?

_____

_____

_____

_____

_____

_____

_____

_____

_____

Your Personal Prayer About Perseverance:

_____

_____

_____

_____

_____

9
LET GRACE SING

On a hot and humid July morning, my daughter and my husband and I found ourselves saying goodbye to our home we had known for the last ten years.

It wasn't just our home we were saying goodbye to; it was our two sons, our family cat and the town we were so familiar with. It was my flowers and gardens which had become my therapy for the past several years. It was there that I found peace and had prayer times with God.

Let Grace Sing | 47

I was saying goodbye to years of history and friendships. My husband was saying goodbye to his job of 30-plus years, and my daughter was leaving the town and community she grew up in.

We had anticipated this move for the past year, because my husband was retiring, and my daughter was graduating high school. Many decisions were being made about colleges and where we would retire. We each felt the call of change beckoning within us.

We knew it would be a move to another state and massive changes would take place. Half the family was moving, and half the family was staying. We would miss each other dreadfully.

The day had finally arrived, and now, here we were with the car loaded up, ready to make the million mile trek, or so it seemed like a million miles anyway. We were excited, anticipatory, nervous and somewhat scared, too. "What did the future hold?" I knew each of us was thinking that. This would be the first time our family would be separated from each other and miles apart at that.

As a Mom, I couldn't resist the thoughts of: "What if they get sick? Will they know what doctor to call? Will they take care of themselves properly? Will they be eating enough and taking their vitamins? Will my daughter have good roommates? Will they be kind? What will her college instructors be like? Will she be safe? What if I don't like my new home or my new neighbors? What if they don't like me?"

Suddenly, I missed my flowers and gardens and my kitty even more. I missed my sons even more, and we weren't even out of the state. Now, I wasn't sure if I wanted my daughter in college or not. "Is she really ready?" I asked myself.

I realized I was saying goodbye and hello at the same time. Goodbye to all that was familiar to me and hello to all that was not familiar to me. I found myself in a conversation with God asking Him that very question. "Please tell me, God, what do I do when I find myself saying goodbye and hello at the same time?"

There were many times in my garden when I prayed and conversed with Him, sharing my cares, concerns and the desires of my heart, that I would get a sense of His loving voice and thoughts towards me. Now, here I was in a packed car with music playing and chatty conversations, and I suddenly heard my Father's loving voice, "Let grace sing. Open the doors and windows of your heart and let grace sing."

I had to meditate on that awhile. What does grace do? How does it sing? How do I open the doors and windows of my heart? My thoughts were brought back to my times spent in the garden. In those times, I came to God with my worries and concerns. In those times, I came to Him with my what-ifs and unknowns of the future.

The grace of His peace would answer me there. Grace would sing me His song of courage and love. It would whisper its melody of peace and trust. Oh yes, I knew this song. This song of grace is the love of God where there is no fear.

I realized at that moment that God meets me wherever I am. Whether I am in my garden, or in a loaded car packed with suitcases, as I sing this song of grace, the what-ifs and the fear of the unknown all become distant shadows.

My family, too, has learned the song of grace. We have learned to open the doors and windows of our hearts to sing this song called grace. It is a simple and humble elegance that dances with us in this journey called life.

Let Grace Sing | 49

*But he answered me, 'My grace is always more than enough
for you,'*

—2 Corinthians 12:9, TPT

Dear Father,

*Thank You for Your gift of grace. Through Jesus and Your love for us,
You have set us free to sing this song of grace. It is grace that doesn't
condemn or bring fear, but it gives courage and peace that empowers
and gives strength.*

We will sing grace with the open doors and windows of our hearts.

Amen.

JOURNAL — Nine

<u>Your Personal Journal:</u>

There are moments in life where we need extended amounts of grace.

What does grace mean to you?

How has it helped and changed you?

_____

_____

_____

_____

_____

_____

_____

_____

_____

<u>Your Personal Prayer:</u>

_____

_____

_____

_____

10

BETRAYAL

*B*etrayal is one of the most disheartening things that can happen to someone. Webster's defines betrayal as this: "Violation of a person's trust, confidence or moral standard. Treacherously abandoned, deserted or mistreated." It leaves one with the consequences of post traumatic stress disorder (PTSD), such as shock, fear and rage. It is emotional trauma that can take years to recover.

Betrayal | 53

I was betrayed by someone when I was a little girl at the young age of eight, as my sexual innocence was violated and stolen from me. Of course, I was told every perpetrator's standard line, "Don't tell anybody." However, as soon as I could get away from them, I immediately told a loved one because I thought I would die, smothered by the weight of it all. I could not get rid of the weight of this awful trespass and violation fast enough.

The urgency to tell my loved one gave me a sense of safety. I longed to hear the words, "It will be okay. You are safe. They will never come near you again. I will take care of this." However, the words I heard were not that. Instead, they were the same as my perpetrator: "Don't tell anybody."

Not only did I feel the pain and heavy weight of betrayal from the agony and confusion of the molestation itself, but I also felt the betrayal of loyalty and protection that should have very well come from a loved one.

So, as an eight year old kid, I did as I was told and never told anyone... for years.

However, the emotional trauma of the betrayal sowed its damaged goods into my life from fear to anger, to unhealthy relationships, to unhealthy habits.

Betrayal is a mean thing. It brings ugly and dark things to its victim, such as confusion, loneliness and fear. It took me years to reckon with this betrayal. A violation done to me when I was too young to even be aware of such a violation.

It wasn't until I was in my thirties with young children of my own when this traumatic event began to unfold itself in my memories. The trauma of the event began to speak its truth to my innermost being, and I couldn't deny my rage, fear, confusion and shame. I couldn't deny my tears and unanswered questions.

I opened up to a friend, but she didn't believe me. She didn't come right out and tell me she didn't believe me, but she didn't have to because her response told me everything I needed to know. She acted angry, questioning me, and then quickly changed the subject, blowing me off. I was hurt and shocked she didn't believe me—a sense of betrayal again from another person I thought I could be safe with. Thank God for my husband who did believe me and loved me through the memories of this trauma.

There are many different kinds of betrayals in life. Isn't it a shame to have to say there are many different kinds of betrayal in life? They usually are from loved ones, close friends, business partners and people in our life whom we trust, hold dear and love.

Betrayal makes us lose our sense of balance. It wounds our feelings of self-worth and self-value. It makes us question our intelligence. It opens the door to anger and fear.

Yes, I have had many betrayals in my life: A business person lied to and cheated me, costing me thousands of dollars. A lifelong friend unfriended me because of my beliefs. Loved ones believed the worst about me and distanced themselves from me.

Betrayal is ugly. It hurts. It wounds. It makes us feel alone and confused. To come to terms with betrayal we must come to terms with ourselves. We must be honest with our feelings of how it has made us feel. Are we angry? Are we sad? Do we feel disgust, shame, fear or rage? We must be truthful to our own selves in how we are feeling if we are going to heal. If we are not, then we are betraying our own selves. We must be completely honest within.

After all, we know the truth of what happened. We know the truth of the betrayal, even if no one else does, or no one else believes us. We must be true to ourselves in identifying what we are feeling and what our emotions are.

Oftentimes when experiencing betrayal, identifying our feelings and emotions can be the most difficult thing to do because betrayal often comes with confusion. Yes, betrayal often brings confusion.

I am not a counselor or a professional, but having gone through this school of hard knocks, I have learned a few things that have helped me overcome the atrocities of betrayal.

The first one is: don't retaliate. It won't get you anywhere except angrier, more hurt and more divisive as a person with less peace. If you're normal, you'll want to retaliate. Your first instinct will most likely be your first response because you have been violated, cheated, lied to and trespassed against. Human nature wants to fight back.

However, you want to break the cycle. To break the cycle of betrayal there must be forgiveness— a letting go. It goes without saying that there will be anger, tears and more anger and more tears. It is a process. Find a trusted friend, partner or counselor who is a good listener, who you can talk to, cry to, and vent your feelings of anger.

Read material that will help you understand your feelings and emotions. Most importantly, go to God and ask Him to heal your mind, will and emotions that you suffered with this betrayal.

Give these perpetrators to God.

Name their names and give them to God.

Forgive them by faith.

Even if you feel you are doing this mechanically, that is ok. Forgiveness and letting go is an act of faith, and God honors this. He knows your heart; He understands your hurt and has compassion on the betrayal that has been done to you.

In one of my conversations with the Lord concerning a very hurtful betrayal, I asked, "Have I forgiven them?"

I sensed the Lord saying this to me, *"I have forgiven them. Now you can forgive them and let them go. Do not think for a moment that I have not seen what they have done to you. I have. I have the grace and love to forgive them. Perhaps you do not. But in Me you have all things, so let them go. Let them go to Me, and you will be free. I will cleanse your heart, heal your soul and renew your mind of all the trauma and pain they have caused you. I have seen it all. I know what it is like to be betrayed. I know the sting, the kiss of betrayal and the darkness it alludes to. You have the grace in Me to let go. Because I love you, I can take the resentment, the anger, the fear, the detriment of all it has caused you. I am the Faithful One. The Safe One. I will never leave you, betray you or forsake you. In Me, you have peace."*

The power of God's love has helped me in dealing with overcoming these betrayals that have happened to me in my life. I believe in being honest with ourselves about the emotions we are faced with when we are betrayed. I also believe in talking with a trusted friend, counselor or partner, and most importantly, having that conversation with God, that you, too, can be healed of the wound of betrayal.

Forgive over and over and you will be forgiven over and over.

—Luke 6:37, TPT

Dear loving and kind Lord,

Where I am weak, You are strong. Where I do not have the power to forgive, You do. Cleanse me and free me from all unforgiveness. Heal me where I need healing. Like the woman who touched the hem of Your garment and was healed, so I reach out to You in faith to heal and restore me from these abuses of betrayals in my life. Thank You for Your love and mercy to me. Thank You that You have begun a good work in me, and You will complete it.

Amen.

JOURNAL — Ten

Your Personal Journal:

The trauma of betrayal often leaves one feeling confused, hurt, lonely, guilty and a variety of other negative emotions. To come to a place of peace, we must come to a place of forgiveness. This, in turn, brings us to a place of letting go. God loves you and wants to heal you from the hurts of betrayal. Talking to a counselor, trusted friend or loved one will help you navigate your emotions. Journaling and writing prayers of expression are also a good source of healing and restoration.

_____

_____

_____

_____

_____

_____

_____

Your Personal Prayer:

_____

_____

_____

_____

_____

11

GUILT

I believe there are two kinds of guilt. There's a good guilt and a bad guilt. A good guilt checks us when we are responsible for an offense of doing something wrong. It could be an offense of breaking a law, lying, or as simple as not bringing that grocery cart back to its proper place and leaving it hanging out in the parking lot! This kind of guilt lets us know that we need to make a wrong, right. This kind of guilt is a check to our character and moral being that we have trespassed a moral and ethical responsibility, and it is our duty to make it right. This is a good guilt. It is set up to make us responsible, healthy people and citizens.

It is the bad guilt, however, that condemns us, robs us and leaves us feeling down.

It leaves us with a false responsibility that we have done something wrong. False guilt can hinder us in many ways. It's an unhealthy response of wanting to please people and compromise our beliefs, responsibilities or our emotional and practical needs. When we do that, we feel guilty, either towards ourselves or towards that individual. The compromise brings the guilt.

For me, it has been letting my mom's phone call go to voicemail. I would beat myself up over this. When the truth of the matter is, I was really busy at the time with my family, job or other responsibilities. Then, if I did answer every phone call, I would be impatient and aggravated with her because I was in the middle of a task. I would feel enormous guilt for being impatient and aggravated. I couldn't win. Either way, I felt guilty, but it was a wrong kind of guilty; it was a self-condemnation type of guilt.

Oftentimes, I would feel guilty saying no to a friend, or taking too long at a checkout line in a store or a bank. If I was running late making supper or doing an errand, I would exhaust myself with more guilt.

Feeling guilt is an unpleasant emotion. It's one thing if you have done something of significant offense, as I mentioned before, in breaking a law, lying or cheating. That guilt is there to set you straight and urge you to make it right. However, when we are feeling the guilt of emotion, when we say no to a family member or friend because we are not able to make a commitment, or simply do not want to make a commitment, we should not feel guilty.

So many of us are carrying around false guilt. I know I have for many years as a child, as an adult and as a mother, wife, daughter, sister and friend. Guilt could've been my middle name. It's a loathsome thing that can weigh us down, suffocating our true potential and personality. We simply were not made to carry around a baggage of false guilt. It may come across as humility, but really it is a false humility. We compromise our own needs and responsibilities to cater to those of others for the sake of not wanting to hurt their feelings.

When we are true to ourselves, then and only then, can we be true to others. When we are true to ourselves and our needs, we build confidence within ourselves. This yields the confidence to be true to others. It builds the confidence to say, "NO," where we need to say, "NO." As we are true to ourselves, we build patience with ourselves, which allows us to give patience to others. As we exercise this practice of being true to ourselves, we gain muscle in our confidence, self-worth and value.

When these areas in our life and character are made stronger, we are able to function in our relationships. Daily tasks are free from forced behavior and responses that we really didn't want to have in the first place. We are free to give right and healthy responses. We are free to say, "yes, no or maybe." We are free to take our time and be patient with ourselves and even make mistakes. We are free from false guilt. I like what Paul says in Romans 8:1, "So now the case is closed. There remains no accusing voice of condemnation against those who are joined in life-union with Jesus, the Anointed One" (TPT).

Because of what Jesus did on the cross for us, we are free from all condemnation. As Jesus Himself has said, "If therefore the Son shall make you free, ye shall be free indeed!" (John 8:36, ASV). This is a wonderful promise. I can have peace in the fact that Jesus has taken all my guilt, all my shame and all my false guilt on the cross and has set me free! May we rest in the truth and assurance of this.

Condemnation and false guilt keeps us away from God and closed off to real, vital, and healthy relationships with people. We are meant to be in thriving and healthy relationships with people and God. In order to be free and healthy in our mind and spirit, we must be free from false guilt, false shame, false accusations and the lies that are holding us back from all that we are meant to be. Give your guilt to God today, lay it down at the cross and know that God is for you, not against you.

Dear Lord,

Heal me of all false guilt and shame. I give to You this baggage that I am not meant to carry. I don't want it. Thank You for the freedom in expressing myself in healthy ways. Thank You for setting me free.

Amen.

JOURNAL — Eleven

<u>Your Personal Journal:</u>

Guilt can be a condemning force.

How does guilt make you feel?

In what ways can you overcome guilt to bring you to a place of peace?

_____

_____

_____

_____

_____

_____

_____

_____

_____

<u>Your Personal Prayer About Guilt:</u>

_____

_____

_____

_____

_____

12

HEAVENLY ENCOUNTERS

My father was a strikingly handsome man with crystal blue eyes, a smile larger than life and a laugh that would engage a whole room. His white silver hair, prominent cheekbones and strong jaw line fared well with his straight-shooter, no-nonsense personality. He stood 6 feet tall, which, at times, seemed so much taller to me. Perhaps it was because he was my Dad, and all Dads appear taller and larger than life sometimes.

Heavenly Encounters | 67

Now, as he lays here in a hospital bed in his living room, in the home I grew up in, I see a different man. He is thin and weak. His crystal blue eyes are grey and fading. His prominent cheekbones are sunken and his strong jawline is... well, not strong.

My mind reminisces of days gone by in this living room where a lifetime of Christmases and birthdays were shared. My memory is full of family gatherings with my dad gleefully laughing, giving the grandchildren piggy back rides throughout the house.

Here he now lays with his lymph nodes swollen, protruding from his body. This time, the family was once again gathered, but not for a joyous occasion. My dad was slipping away. My strong, beautiful and handsome Dad would soon be saying goodbye to us.

He had been wrestling with lymphoma cancer for the past 18 months, and he was losing the wrestling match. He fought it, and he fought it hard. Being the straight shooter he was, he had asked the doctor months before how much time he had. I remember well when Dad came to my house to tell me.

It was a Saturday morning, a brisk morning with bright sunshine as my Dad, armed with groceries, entered my home. Saturdays were special. Dad always came with several bags of groceries. I never knew what the grocery bags would be; it was always a fun surprise for us! It would range from huge cans of olive oil to vitamins, to large containers of laundry soap, to fresh cut meat from the butcher or local fish store.

This Saturday, however, was different. The groceries were just as varied, but he seemed more serious than normal. He was a matter of fact person, so it was no surprise to me when he got straight to the point. Dad told me rather firmly that he had just a matter of months to live. He then handed me a paper of all the details of his arrangements. He gave me no time or allowance to cry, mourn or share grief. He was not about that, and he did not want any pity, sorrow or hugs. I knew he was trying to protect me this way by not giving way to these emotions. He then told me how to cook this certain brand of fish he bought, then turned to the grandkids with his large smile and laugh as he hugged them goodbye.

He was now slipping into unconsciousness as my husband, Mom and I said our goodbyes. As I squeezed his hand tightly, I told him how proud I was of him—a strong, loving, brave father and person. I told him how smart, intelligent and how handsome he was. My mother tenderly and softly wept as she told him it was okay to let go. She assured him that she would be okay and safe and that he could let go now. My husband held his arm and reassured him that we would all meet him in heaven one day. At that moment, a tear made its way down my father's cheek, and he let go.

He was gone. It was a sacred moment in this living room. Perhaps a more sacred moment than all the others shared.

My grief for him lingered on for days. The days turned into weeks. I knew in my head that my father was no longer in pain, no longer suffering, no longer too weak to eat or drink or laugh his hearty laugh, but my heart just couldn't accept it.

Night after night, I would lay in bed in grief. After a full day of responsibilities, errands and taking care of the kids, as soon as my head would hit the pillow, the grief would come full force. The tears would stream down my face, and I would see my dad in that hospital bed suffering.

Finally, one night as I prayed, I asked the Lord to please take my grieving heart. "Please let me know my Dad is okay, Lord. Please let me know that he is not suffering anymore." These

Heavenly Encounters | 69

were the prayers of my heart. I just had to know. That night my prayer was answered. The Lord spoke to me through a dream.

In the dream, my family and I were gathered in my parent's kitchen. My Aunt, my father's sister, who happened to be born exactly one year apart from him, sharing the same birthday, had passed away several years before, was also there. She looked well and healthy with her skin aglow. Also, a dear, loving friend and neighbor of my parents was there in our midst. She too, had passed several years ago, dying tragically and suddenly. She was there, radiant with joy and peace. We were all in the kitchen laughing, joking and having a wonderful time. It was a time of celebration. There was so much joy.

My father was in a navy blue suit, looking so handsome. He was the epitome of health. His smile was large, and his eyes were the most fabulous blue I had ever seen. They radiated beams of light. He stood tall and strong. We were all telling him how wonderful it was to see him and how wonderful he looked. His face glistened as he spoke, and his eyes had beams of light shining forth from them, lighting up the whole room.

As he told us how happy and excited he was to be with us, we could all reach out and touch the joy that was in that room. It radiated and bounced off of each one of us. My Dad then told us that he could only stay awhile with us and that he had just come down to tell us that he was alright. He said he needed to go back up, and he exclaimed with great joy that he was fine now—happy and healthy—and that all was okay! We were holding champagne glasses, and we all raised them up and said, "Cheers!" with great jubilee in our midst.

My dream then ended. I woke up smiling, laughing and crying. I woke up happy.

70 | PATHWAYS TO PEACE

I knew that I knew that my father was better than better—he was fine, healthy, whole and complete. My heart of grief had been healed, and I knew that my father's well-being had been healed as well. My innermost being had rest now, as did my father's. We were both restored.

O death, where is thy sting? O grave, where is thy victory?

—1 Corinthians 15:55, KJV

Dear God,

Thank You for healing us in times of grief. It is too much to bear the weight of grief. We need Your perspective and truths during these times of hurt and sorrow to set us free. Thank You that You care and understand. We are grateful that You heal our hurting hearts during these times. Oh death, where is your sting? Jesus takes it into His hands. You take that sting away from our hearts and those of our loved ones as You grant us new eternal life in You.

Amen.

JOURNAL —Twelve

<u>Your Personal Journal:</u>

Grief is an emotion of deep sadness to be reckoned with. God understands our grief. His great love for us desires that we have peace and healing in our grief. It is my prayer that your grief be healed with a touch of the Father's love.

_____

_____

_____

_____

_____

_____

_____

_____

_____

<u>Your Personal Prayer:</u>

_____

_____

_____

_____

13

WHERE THE HOMELESS LIVE

As we pulled into the gas station, I noticed a young man sitting on the curb, head down, with his bike laid down on the pavement next to him. It was early in the morning, and he got my attention by the way he looked—stringy hair, dirty clothes and sorrow was on his face.

At the time, my husband and I had been doing some traveling for our company and we were in our vehicle for hours at a

Where the Homeless Live | 73

time. I always packed a small cooler with water, snacks and fruit. I asked my husband to stop the vehicle.

As I rolled down my window, I held out a bottle of water and asked the young man if he wanted it. "Yes, thank you," he said. He appeared to be in his early twenties. As I asked him his name, I reached for a banana from our cooler and some cash in my purse. I only had a dollar or two on me, but as I handed it to him, I asked him his story.

He excitedly, desperately, asked me, "Would you mind if I eat this banana right now?" He told me he had been living on the streets this past year since both of his parents died in an accident. He had become addicted to meth and was trying to quit, but he was having a hard time. All I could see was the sorrow in his sunken eyes and the hurt in his voice as he told me his story.

His name was Matthew. I told Matthew that his name meant "gift from God." I told him that his life didn't end here. God loved him ever so much and had a destiny, future and hope for him. I asked Matthew if I could pray for him. "Please do" was his response. He bowed his head and as I prayed, tears came to his eyes. I prayed that God would show him the way, the truth, the life, and set him free from his addiction. I told him God had good things for him.

He thanked me for the bottle of water, banana and the few dollars I had given him, then he wearily rode off on his dilapidated bike. I thought about Matthew often after this encounter, praying for him to have a better life. How special he was to God and how desperately he needed to know that.

Later that day, as my husband and I were unloading our van at our hotel parking lot, my attention was drawn to a young woman pushing her bike on the sidewalk next to us. She was in her early 40's, or maybe in her 30's.

It is difficult to tell their age when they are homeless because their skin looks much older than what it really is. Sun damage takes its toll as does the weather elements of the wind, rain and colder temperatures.

I would come to learn her name was Christi. She had hard lines around her eyes which spoke of her rough living. Her hair was held in an elastic; looking greasy, sticky and matted in places. Her black mascara was rubbed around her eyes from not being able to wash for days, I imagine.

She had plastic bags attached to the handlebars of her bike and she was carrying a dirty, raggedy backpack. She pushed her bicycle with weariness and sweat dripping down her face. It was 102 degrees outside. The intense sun was beating her down, even more than her current situation. I grabbed an ice cold water bottle from our cooler with a few dollars and chased her down. Our conversation went something like this.

"Hey, hey, how ya doin?" (I always feel somewhat awkward approaching the homeless because for me, it *is* awkward. I can't imagine their predicament, living life this way.)

"Uh, ummm ok, I guess."

"Where ya goin?"

"I'm going back to Washington to be with my kids. My husband left me."

"Are you homeless?"

"Yes."

"What's your name?"

Where the Homeless Live | 75

"Christi. My name is Christi."

I handed Christi the bottle of water and the few dollars I had on me. She cracked opened the bottle of water and guzzled it down.

"Thank you," she said.

"Can I pray for you Christi? Do you mind if I pray for you?"

"Yes. Yes. Please, do."

And then, as I was praying for Christi, with my hand on her shoulder, I found myself silently praying for me. Show me what to pray, Lord. What does she need? Show me how to pray for this woman.

I began to pray for God to bless her, to heal her where she needed healing. To physically and emotionally heal her heart and well-being. I prayed that where she felt betrayed and hurt, for God to go to those places and heal her. I asked God to send helpers to Christi and to keep her safe.

Christi's eyes began to tear up and she said, "You know, I've been mad at God."

I said, "Yeah, I've been mad at God at times, too. I think if we're honest with ourselves, we all get mad at God sometimes. But God loves you. He understands. He knows. I may not know your story, Christi, but God does and He cares, and He understands. I don't know your story Christi and you don't know mine. We don't know each other's story, but God does."

Christi began to tell me, "It's hell out there and not safe." She tells me how truly scared she is and has to find her way home. I'm listening because it seems that is all I can do: listen. I listen with my heart, my ears and my eyes fully engaged because that is all I really have to offer. As she gets ready to load up on her

76 | PATHWAYS TO PEACE

bike, I tell Christi to be safe; that I hear and understand what she is saying. I pray again for her and for her safety and well-being. As I leave her, I tell her God loves her.

"Thank you. Yes. Thank you," she says. They always say, "Thank you."

As we parted ways, I had tears in my eyes, and she had tears in hers. I didn't want to cry in front of her because she did not need pity—she needed courage. She was in need of empowerment with empathy and compassion.

Every time when I encounter the homeless, my heart is broken. As I pray for them, hear their story, give them a cold bottle of water and a few dollars, I feel better. I don't feel as helpless. I feel like I am helping them and it makes me feel good. So, I realize I do this for myself as much as I do it for them. It is for both of us.

I approach the homeless in my weakness of not knowing how to approach them each time. I don't always do it in full confidence of knowing exactly what to say or what to pray. I don't have much to offer them either, except a few dollars, a prayer, a bottle of water and some fruit or snacks. I am careful as to who not to approach because many are in a rage with unpredictable anger.

I know that Christy and Matthew were both thankful for the prayer and the nice cold bottle of water. Thankful for the few dollars and fruit, but even more, I believe they were thankful for the conversation. They were thankful for someone to talk to them, someone to listen to them and someone to look them in the eyes. They were thankful for someone who didn't look at them with shame, discord or disgust.

I found it interesting that, when Christi told me she was mad at God at times, I responded to her that I understood, "Yes, I, too, have felt mad at God at times." She got quiet. Real quiet, as if she was so surprised to hear that. Here I was with clean hair, clean clothes and makeup nicely done, and I'm telling her, in all honesty, that, yes, I've felt that way before, too. That was a profound, pivotal moment for me and perhaps, for Christi, too.

The truth of the matter is this. No matter how I look, or how you look, we do not know each other's story. We don't know the detrimental parts of each other's story. My hell, your hell, we don't know each other's story, and very few take the time or heart to really listen. The other truth to the matter is that God does.

I hope that if Matthew and Christi received anything that day, more than the banana, bottled water or those few dollars, I hope they received that God knows, God listens, God cares and that God loves them.

And the King will answer them, 'Don't you know? When you cared for one of the least important of these my little ones, my true brothers and sisters, you demonstrated love for me.'

—Matthew 25:40, TPT

~

Dear God,

Thank You for Your love for us. In this world that can be so harsh and unkind, it is Your love that is gentle and forgiving. Thank You that Your love, Oh God, is a safe place for us to go in times of trouble. May You bring more help to the homeless and answer their prayers and cries for help. May they know that You are a loving and kind God.

Amen.

JOURNAL — Thirteen

<u>Your Personal Journal:</u>

Journal your thoughts about "Where the Homeless Live."

In these plights of society, how can we be the helpers?

_____

_____

_____

_____

_____

_____

_____

_____

_____

_____

<u>Your Personal Prayer:</u>

_____

_____

_____

_____

_____

14

BEAUTY IN THE DESERT

When we think of the desert, images of sand, dust and isolation may come to mind. In the desert are extreme weather changes as well. Sand storms, drought and extreme temperatures are the desert's personality. During the day, it is visited by extreme heat, and at night, the heat escapes to coldness. Places of the desert seem forsaken or abandoned and perhaps, many are.

Beauty in the Desert | 81

During a recent visit to Death Valley, I saw firsthand the beauty and the barrenness of the desert. I saw the beautiful sand dunes and amazing rock formations. With each twisting turn and elevation, the desert had a changing landscape, much to my surprise. I did not expect the beauty I saw. There was beauty in the rocks, sands and elevation of looking high and low.

Oftentimes in our life of what could be called a desert season, we experience the difficulty of extreme temperatures. The heat of the day is so uncomfortable, and the cold of the night is almost unbearable. Sometimes with the varying temperatures, we don't know how to adjust and confusion sets in. We feel disoriented with the heat and uncomfortable with the cold. Life is like that. During these desert times it is easy to feel abandoned, uncared for, unnoticed and isolated.

When I first left home at the age of 19, I thought I was ready to face the world. I felt independent and confident I could manage on my own. I was not prepared for my desert times, in which great feelings of homesickness and loneliness came upon me.

I was far away from my New England home where I had grown up. Where I moved to was a thousand miles away from my little town in Connecticut. The culture was different, the food was different, the landscape and temperatures were different. At times, many times, I felt alone, scared and isolated. At times, I felt misunderstood, rejected and mistreated.

"This is supposed to be good for me?" I questioned. "I'm supposed to thrive here?" I cried. I walked alone to class many times. I sat alone in class many times. I was alone many times.

What I didn't realize was that inside of me, that little seed of my future, destiny and purpose was being watered and nurtured. It

82 | PATHWAYS TO PEACE

was developing, growing, stretching and reaching new heights. Even in this desert land, I was thriving.

Often in our desert times, in the driest times of our life, we feel we are in a wasteland. Our dreams and desires seem lost. Confusion fogs our vision. People and friends don't understand. Perhaps even some relationships come to end and are broken.

Desert times are not really fun times. The temperatures vary from day to day and shift from night to night. We feel we have lost our sense of balance because of the new lows and varying elevations. We cannot see the beauty around us or within us because of the sandstorms that blind and hinder our vision. We have to carefully watch where we walk so we don't walk into a prickly cactus or slithering poisonous snake. The desert season is there to teach us many things about ourselves and about the life around us. I faced other desert seasons in my life besides those of my college days. The seasons of desert times where I felt alone, isolated and barren would come and go.

I remember during one such time of walking through this desert season of my life while at college, I saw a storm brewing across the way. As it got closer and closer, the sky got darker and darker. I was walking with my roommate across a parking lot, heading to our apartment when the clouds opened, and the heavens let down a torrential rain pour. We began running, trying to outrun the rain, but to no avail. The rain came down harder and harder in bucketfuls. Our running soon turned into jumping into the huge rain puddles. We laughed like two little kids jumping, splashing and running in the rain. It was so much fun! We were soaked and drenched, but it felt so good! Sooner or later the rains do come in our desert time. The purpose of the desert has been formed within us, giving way to beauty.

Beauty in the Desert | 83

During my visit to Death Valley, I was reminded of this. Between the rocks and sand, stone and parched land, there are beautiful flowers tucked in their midst. One particular one caught my eye. Its beauty stood out in a magnificent way. There it was in a hard, parched land, giving way to a brilliant yellow. Fluorescent in color, lovingly facing the sun, it reminded me once again that there is beauty in the desert. I posted a picture of these flowers above.

> *The wilderness and dry land will be joyously glad! The desert will blossom like a rose and rejoice! Every dry and barren place will burst forth with abundant blossoms, dancing and spinning with delight!*

> —Isaiah 35:1-2, TPT

Dear Father,

Maker of heaven and earth, thank You for the beauty in the desert.

Amen.

JOURNAL — Fourteen

<u>Your Personal Journal:</u>

Often in our desert times, in the most dry or barren times of our life, we feel we are in a wasteland. Our dreams and desires seem lost, but there is beauty in the desert and soon a flower blooms.

And let us not be weary in well doing: for in due season we shall reap, if we faint not.

—Galatians 6:9, KJV

God is not finished with you yet. You have so much more to give, to receive, to learn and to grow. In what ways will you motivate, nourish and refresh yourself?

_____

_____

_____

_____

_____

<u>Your Personal Prayer:</u>

_____

_____

_____

_____

15

THE ARTIST

My journey on this particular day took me to higher elevations than I had never experienced before. It was a clear day with majestic skies of blue. The air felt fresh and clean, invigorating to my senses. As we journeyed on, the overview became increasingly interesting with remarkable scenery.

The Artist | 87

The rock formations and towering trees were proudly displaying their beauty. The twist and turns of the road and the heights of where we were grabbed my attention.

As I tried to appreciate all the beautiful scenery, I could not be more aware that one false move and I'd be toppling over the ledge with no one finding us. The height of the elevations frightened me, since I had never been to those kinds of heights before. As I looked out the passenger window, I could not help but look thousands of feet below to a very steep landing. The beauty was engaging but so were the depths and heights of where we were going.

We had several more miles to go as the road got steeper and the elevations got higher. I really wasn't prepared for the heights of this journey or the many twists and turns in the road. I had no choice but to continue on our journey in order to reach our destination. We were now reaching an elevation of 9,000 feet, and just as I had decided that I didn't want to go much higher, there was a turn in the road. As we decided to take the turn to rest from our journey, a remarkable surprise greeted us.

It was one of the most spectacular sights I have ever seen in my lifetime; the beauty was captivating. It left me speechless for several moments. All I could do was gaze around me, stretching my eyesight to focus as far as I could possibly see, not wanting to miss one hidden glance of beauty. The glistening blue waters reflecting the snow capped Rocky Mountains appeared as the most beautiful mirror. The fabulous blue sky was showing off its magnificence as heavenly as it possibly could. The snow covered ice on the waters looked magical and perfect.

It was a sight to behold. I wanted to keep this vision in my mind's eye forever. I had no idea my journey would lead me to this most beautiful place on this day.

As I was taking in the scenery around me, I could not help but notice a talented artist down below by the mesmerizing blue lake. He was also taking in the beauty of this majestic place of crystal blue waters, towering snow capped mountains and glorious blue skies. It was then that I was humbly reminded of the greatest artist of all, the Creator of heaven and earth, and the glorious works of His hands.

Suddenly, the twists and turns of the narrow road I was journeying on that brought me here weren't such a threat. The high elevations were no longer a scary point of view for me. The distractions of the journey were soon forgotten. Perhaps that is the Master Artist's plan all along: to bring us to a pathway of peace with such beauty and loveliness. A place in our journey to realize that life is so much larger than worry, petty differences and a fear of unknown heights. A place where we can relax to enjoy the perfect moments of gratitude and beauty that is in our midst.

To go where the peace is, we sometimes have to follow a pathway that is uncomfortable. Perhaps it is a pathway with twists and turns and heights we aren't comfortable climbing. Yet, when we arrive at our destination, we see that the Master Artist's hand was involved the whole time, creating a beautiful resting place for us, a place of beauty and peace.

> *Ah Lord God! behold, thou hast made the heaven and the earth by thy great power and stretched out arm, and there is nothing too hard for thee.*
>
> —Jeremiah 32:17, KJV

The Artist | 89

Dear Father,

Thank You for the plans of beauty and rest You have for us as we travel along on this journey of life. Your provision of blue skies, glorious mountains and refreshing waters give us peace and joy. O Lord, how majestic are the works of Your hands! You are the Master Artist captivating us with Your beauty. I am grateful.

Amen.

JOURNAL — Fifteen

<u>Your Personal Journal:</u>

The beauty of nature heals and refreshes our soul. It rejuvenates us and brings peace to our innermost being. The artistry of God's handiwork is mesmerizing.

Where are some beautiful places of nature that captivate you?

_____

_____

_____

_____

_____

_____

_____

_____

<u>Your Personal Prayer:</u>

_____

_____

_____

_____

16

A FATHER

I had always been a lover of God and considered myself to be in a relationship with Him through prayer and Bible reading. However, there was this unhealthy fear of God that hung out with me, along with a shadow of condemnation. I had an underlying feeling and emotion of never feeling quite good enough, never feeling completely accepted by His love. I saw Him more stern, rather than tender-loving and absolutely caring.

Understanding the fatherhood of God changed my life. It gave me a prayer life where I could go to Him in transparency without the fear of condemnation and judgment. Instead of visualizing a stern God somewhere up there ready to slam down the gavel at my smallest little mistake or sin, I saw a loving Father who endeared me and One Who was patient and kind.

A father's love is one that meets the needs of the family. It nurtures, it faces challenges responsibly and it gives unconditional love. It provides financially for food warmth and shelter. A father's love gives good counsel and advice. It is a love that has open arms of forgiveness. It yields faith and courage to its family. He shows loving discipline when needed to give guidance and respect. A father's love also knows how to have fun, excitement, adventure and healthy challenges, too. A father's love for the family is a backbone for their stability and well-being.

It also has a huge part in our lives in how we relate to authority figures. We see this in our society with many fatherless children growing up into adulthood angry, not really knowing their identity of worth, value and self-esteem. Their growth, emotionally and in their demeanor, can be stunted and is reflected in how they show self-respect and respect to others.

Earthly fathers are not perfect, nor will they ever be. They have many responsibilities and big shoes to fill to meet all of their family's needs—emotional, physical, financial, psychological, parental, and relational. The greatest quality a father can have for his family is that of love. An emotional bond is so important for the father and child relationship to thrive. To have a healthy, satisfying and stable father and child relationship, there must be hugs, laughs and tears. There must be sharing of emotional moments where the hearts are connected.

My father was a good father. He went to work every day, paid the bills and was responsible for caring for his family. I knew he loved me and that he would always protect me. Our emotional connection, however, was distant. There wasn't a conversation about my feelings or emotions if I was facing a difficult time. I didn't feel freedom emotionally to express myself and neither did he. Many of my friends were "Daddy's Girl," a concept I wanted but a reality I didn't have. I kind of always felt my father was mad at me, disappointed in me, or didn't quite like me enough.

He was a stoic man with a stern personality. Even though I knew he loved me, growing up with an emotional distance from him left me with an emotional void. I wanted to run up into his lap as a little girl and have him smother me with hugs and kisses. I wanted to cry to him as a teenager when I had my first breakup with a boyfriend. I wanted to just be myself, relax and talk about "stuff."

The emotional freedom was just not there. Don't get me wrong, I have the utmost respect for my father and the hard work he invested in his family. The obstacles for a father can be so immense with trying to provide for a family. Perhaps their own life's heartaches and hardships have them withdrawn emotionally.

The perception of my father changed as I saw him change during my child bearing years. I began to see his father's heart as he would play with my children, give them piggyback rides and hold them when they cried. I saw an emotional connection taking place between him and my children which, in turn, helped heal the voided places in my heart.

An emotional disconnect with a father leads to an emotional disconnect with God. It may leave us feeling like he isn't really all that interested in our life's happenings. It may be having us believe that he doesn't really care all that much, or that he is constantly disappointed with us. The truth is that God does not have a gavel waiting to throw down on us. He has a heart of the Father, ready to love, help, nourish and care for us.

He does not have obstacles to overcome in His love for us. We are His heart's desire. He embraces us fully and completely just as we are. We are His children and He is our father, a perfect love that casts out all fear.

> *For the Holy Spirit makes God's fatherhood real to us as he whispers into our innermost being, 'You are God's beloved child!'*
>
> —Romans 8:16, TPT

Dear Father,

How great is Your love for me that I am Your child. Your love for me is without obstacles and with full embrace. Heal me from trauma and emotional voids of the past so that I may embrace Your fatherhood completely. Your love for me as Your child is steadfast and true, lacking no good thing, and I am loved by You.

Amen.

JOURNAL — Sixteen

<u>Your Personal Journal:</u>

An emotional disconnect with a father leads to an emotional disconnect with God.

Name ways you see God as your loving Father.

_____

_____

_____

_____

_____

_____

_____

_____

_____

_____

<u>Your Personal Prayer:</u>

_____

_____

_____

_____

_____

17

THE POWER OF SELF-ACCEPTANCE

I was elated with excitement to meet my new friends as I sat in the front row seat of my first grade class. I could not wait to learn to read and write. My mom had curled my hair the night before with pretty pink sponge rollers, and we picked out the perfect dress that I thought looked very grown up for a first grader. I wanted everything to be perfect for this special first day of school. I wanted to be well prepared, so I wore a bright smile and carried a happy attitude ready to give it my all.

The Power of Self-Acceptance | 99

Soon though, I quickly found out that many of my classmates could count higher numbers than me. They could also recite the alphabet quicker and faster than I could. Some even knew how to read sentences and find number pages in the reading book.

For this, I was not prepared. I overheard some of the classmates asking each other where they went to kindergarten. One pretty and perfect little girl turned to me and asked me where I went to kindergarten. I meekly told her and all the other inquisitive listening ears that I didn't go to kindergarten. Some of the kids snickered as I sheepishly looked away.

Self-acceptance is such an added necessity in life. At that time, many children didn't go to kindergarten. It wasn't a prerequisite for first grade. Most public schools did not offer kindergarten then. The children who did attend had their mom's drive them to the local church or a nearby community center. My mom didn't have her license to drive, so I didn't attend kindergarten.

Therefore, I didn't have a head start with numbers, the alphabet, reading or writing. This put me in a very precarious situation. I felt embarrassed at times when I couldn't get to the page number fast enough or write my letters perfect enough. Thank God, I had such an eagerness to learn. I loved reading so much and felt so proud when the teacher would choose me to read aloud to the class, but my self-acceptance was wounded that first day of school. I thought I was different, or less adequate, because so many of my classmates were further along.

What I didn't realize at that time was that our self-acceptance is always tested. There will always be someone smarter, prettier, more athletic, more this and more that than we ourselves are. And that is OKAY. In our growing up years, as a teen facing identity crisis, or as a new fledgling college student, our self-acceptance will be challenged. In the workplace, as a new bride and even in our own families with siblings, our self-acceptance is to be reckoned with.

I was always one with a sensitive nature. I was often told it was a negative character flaw. So, for years, I would try not to be sensitive. It was not who I was though. In trying not to be sensitive, I was not being honest with myself or with others for that matter. Once I learned it was OKAY to be sensitive, I was able to relax, be myself and accept myself.

I learned how to navigate my sensitivity for the good. I realized that sensitivity is a really good thing in this world. I nurtured my sensitivity and approved of it. Self-acceptance is a key to peace. We all want to be accepted. Being at peace with oneself is to accept one's self.

The big change for me began when I realized that I was accepted and loved by God. His love for each of us is unconditional. He knows my flaws, shortcomings, strengths and weaknesses. If He can love and accept me the way I am, knowing all this about me, then surely I can love and accept myself.

He hath made us accepted in the Beloved.

—Ephesians 1:6, KJV

Once we accept this truth in our hearts, that we are accepted and loved by God, we are then free to accept and love ourselves. With this realization in our hearts and well-being, we are now free to accept and love others as well. This is how we change the world. By loving ourselves, flaws and all, we can now go out in the world to love and accept others.

The pathway to having peace with ourselves is self-acceptance. It is a lifelong lesson, one that greets us at all ages of life. Along

The Power of Self-Acceptance | 101

the way, we better ourselves as we grow and learn the lessons of self-acceptance.

It was many years ago that I sat in that first grade class with the unsettled feeling of wanting to be accepted. Those feelings have come and gone many times in my life. I am learning that the peace resides within me. It is called self-acceptance.

For I am fearfully and wonderfully made.

—Psalm 139:14, ASV

Dear God,

Thank You that You accept me just the way I am. I am beloved in Your eyes.

Thank You for Your unconditional love for me.

Amen.

JOURNAL — Seventeen

<u>Your Personal Journal:</u>

It is too easy to compare ourselves to others. God sees you as you are, "fearfully and wonderfully made." You are "His beloved."

Reflect on a time when you were hard on yourself and self-rejecting. How did that make you feel?

_____

_____

_____

_____

_____

_____

_____

_____

_____

<u>Your Personal Prayer:</u>

_____

_____

_____

_____

18

THE DAY THE WORLD STOPPED

*A*s I walked into the grocery store, dressed with my tight fitting mask and reaching for my sanitized grocery cart, I realized my glasses were all steamed up. I had a difficult time focusing, not only with my eyes, but with my mind, heart and soul, too. We were edging our way into nearly a month of self-isolation or "quarantine," as the news stations were calling it. Life as we knew it had changed dramatically. We were not allowed to go out in public, but most public places were closed anyway. The grocery stores were open

The Day the World Stopped | 105

during certain hours, but the only thing was, many of the aisles were empty.

Paper goods were nowhere to be found, and if they were, only a certain limit was allowed. It was the first time I have ever seen no meat at the meat department. Restaurants, places of worship, shopping centers, schools, colleges and beaches were all closed.

A deadly, most hideous virus known as the Coronavirus had invaded the nation, as well as many other nations, and its evil was wreaking havoc. Thousands upon thousands of lives were lost, and many more were ill in self-quarantine or on ventilators. As a nation, we had never been through this before. We were being faced with an unprecedented time. Fear was gripping the country, from young children who really did not understand the disruption of their lives, to the senior citizens who were vulnerable. Fear was laying siege to our peace.

It is interesting to me that at the time of writing this book, *Window Box Series, Pathways to Peace*, our country is faced with a deadly pandemic, seeking answers and solutions. We are in desperate need of a *Pathway to Peace*. First and foremost, medical answers and solutions are needed, but we also need peace of mind—peace to get us through another day of unrelenting somber news and sustain us with strength, vigor and courage.

Peace is a key ingredient in getting through difficult and trying times. It strengthens and gives courage to get us through the toughest places. Peace is a sustaining power. However, the key to attaining it is not always easy.

Time and time again, I find during difficult and trying times in my life, when I turn to the promises of God, it is then that I am on a pathway to peace. Who knows better than God to comfort our heart. As David cries out in the Psalms, "Whom have I in heaven but thee?" (73:25, KJV). In times of isolation and fear, in times of desperation, we find ourselves crying out to God; He is our resolve and hope. Even when everything around us looks bleak and dark, fearful and desolate, we can rest assured that the God of heaven and earth sees it all.

His promise to us, as spoken in Jeremiah 29:11, is that of a hope, a future and a purpose. This is a promise to us individually and a promise to all nations, as well.God's thoughts are not our thoughts, nor His ways, our ways. Our thoughts and ways are finite. They may consist of fear, doubt and drudgery. God's thoughts and ways are so much higher, trustworthy and valid, full of love and peace.

So, as I grab my mask for this week's grocery run, I am realizing the world may seem stopped as I know it, but not as God knows it. His ways are higher than mine. His thoughts are infinite, not finite.

As I quiet myself, I hear His whisper, "Be still and know that I am God." My pathway to peace is to quiet myself and rest in His promises.

Be still, and know that I am God.

—Psalm 46:10, KJV

Thou wilt guide me with thy counsel, And afterward receive me to glory. Whom have I in heaven but thee? And there is none upon earth that I desire besides thee. My flesh and my heart faileth; but God is the strength of my heart and my portion forever.

—Psalm 73:24-26, KJV

Dear Lord,

Thank You that we can trust in You in these particular moments in time. Your plans for us as a people and nation is one of hope, future and destiny. Your thoughts towards us are of love, peace and goodness. Our world may have stopped as we know it, but not as You know it. Your thoughts are higher than ours and Your ways are so much better. Whom have we in heaven but You and we will trust in You.

Amen.

JOURNAL — Eighteen

<u>Your Personal Journal:</u>

The world can be distracting and disheartening at times.

How do you find peace in trying times?

In what ways can you help and heal yourself and those around you?

_____

_____

_____

_____

_____

_____

_____

_____

_____

<u>Your Personal Prayer:</u>

_____

_____

_____

_____

19

MELODY

*A*s I knelt with my young daughter next to her bed to pray (as we did every night), she asked me to pray with her for a kitty. I knelt with her next to her bed, as we had done many nights before, and listened to her sweet little four year old voice pray: "Dear God, please bring me the kitty of my dreams. I want a kitty sooo bad. Thank you, Jesus. Amen."

I prayed with her in faith, wanting to believe with her. I didn't want to shoot her faith down or the precious desire of her

Melody | 111

heart, so I prayed with my sweet little girl each night that she would receive this special kitty she longed for.

Our miniature collie of 16 years had just recently passed away, and we were not ready for another member of the family at this time. Growing up, our family never had a cat, and actually, I wasn't very fond of them. As time went on, my daughter became increasingly persistent, and she would show me pretty little kitties in story books and lure me into pet stores to look at the "pretty, furry kittens." I found myself buying her cute little shirts with kitties on them and cute little stuffed animal kitties of all colors, shapes and sizes. The theme of her message to me was becoming increasingly clear.

A few years passed and the night time ritual of praying for a kitty remained, only with more passion. "Pleeeze dear God, are You hearing my prayers, Jesus? I know You're up there! I know You have a kitty for me! Where is my kitty?" I had one eye open, one eye closed, as I looked at her little determined face grimacing up towards heaven.

Finally, the research began. She investigated animal shelters about how and where to adopt a precious kitty of her own. She also volunteered at an animal shelter where she could learn more about the desire of her heart, her very own kitty. She bought books on how to take care of cats and would follow me room to room, reading me instructions on cat care, while promising me she will take full responsibility.

During this time, our family was going through some difficult situations. These difficulties brought much stress to our home. It was taking a toll on all of us and I could see it affecting my daughter as well. I had read how having an animal could help a young child deal with stress. I had also read that the caring and nurturing for a beloved pet helps comfort and reduce anxiety in children.

112 | PATHWAYS TO PEACE

I was now considering this may be a really good thing for my daughter, but what about me? I didn't need more stress. I did not know how to take care of a cat, much less, like one.

One night after supper, my daughter came to me, asking me to go to the computer with her. She wanted to show me something very special and important to her. She pulled up a chair for me to sit down and look at the information she was about to show me.

Lo and behold, she had found her kitty. I could see it in her eyes; she was totally in love. I have to admit, it was one of the most precious little kitties I had ever seen. You see, all those night time prayers had changed my heart. I didn't realize it until that moment.

Faith is like that. It grows and grows, even when we aren't realizing it. I was praying and agreeing each night with my daughter, no matter how small or how large my faith was. Hers was huge and she was believing that someday she would get this kitty if she kept praying. And pray she did. This led to more praying and researching and activating her faith by volunteering at a shelter to learn more about cats and animals.

All the time, I watched her never give up on her dream. I couldn't help believing with her in my own heart, praying to God my own prayer of: "Anything is possible with You, God. Change my heart."

You may think it's a silly prayer, but when it comes to my kids, I am willing to pray anything! So I prayed, "You know I know nothing about cats, God, and I'm not really a lover of cats, so I'm going to need You to change my heart."

You see, when we are willing to be willing, God can do amazing things in our heart. And so it was, my heart was changed. This particular shelter, where my daughter's dream kitty was

Melody | 113

located, was more than an hour from our home. The next night my daughter, husband and I took the journey to find our special kitten who was only a few weeks old. I could sense the excitement and anticipation of my daughter and in all of us!

As we walked through the doors of the shelter, we saw there were sweet little kitties in various places. My daughter spotted hers immediately and went running to her like it was a long lost reunion. She scooped the little kitten up in her arms as tears of joy filled my eyes. This was a long time coming—years of prayers, yet perfect timing.

Bundled up in a little blanket, my daughter cradled the small kitten in her arms as they sat together in the backseat of our car. I could hear my daughter talking sweetly and softly to the little kitten, giving her all the love she possibly could. Yet, the little kitten kept crying.

The small kitty was scared and shaking. After all, she was just taken away from all she'd known so far: her mama, siblings and all her other little friends. As my daughter sensed the little kitten's fears and tears, she began to sing to her.

As she would sing a soft, sweet song, the kitty would quiet herself. When she would stop, the kitty would once again begin to cry. Again, my daughter would begin her sweet soothing song and our newest little member of the family would quiet down.

This continued all the way home for the hour long drive. Upon reaching home, we still had not chosen a name for the new member of our family. She was a black and white fluffy, part Turkish angora, with beautiful markings. Each of us thought of many different names, yet none quite suited her. The little kitty began to cry again so my daughter once again began to sing to her.

It was at that moment that my daughter happily exclaimed, "I know her name! It is perfect for her! I will name her Melody, because every time I sing to her and make a melody, she stops crying!" So it was, the newest member of our family would be named Melody!

We call Melody our angel kitty because to us, she has brought a melody. Adopting Melody changed our lives that day. She eased the stress in our home with her sweet ways of playing, cuddling and purring. She brought each of us great comfort with her loving ways. She became a best friend to my daughter as they nurtured and cared for one another.

You can't have a melody without harmony. The harmony was the prayers my daughter prayed each night for the desires of her heart. God knew. God heard. He brought Melody at just the right time. We are so thankful for our angel kitty. In our heart is a Melody.

Make God the utmost delight and pleasure of your life, and he will provide for you what you desire the most.

—Psalm 37:4, TPT

Dear Father,

Thank You that You know and care about the desires of our heart. You are faithful to meet them as we keep our eyes upon You.

We love You.

Amen.

JOURNAL — Nineteen

Your Personal Journal:

Melody has brought our family such love and comfort; we call her our Angel Kitty.

Do you have a beloved pet?

How has your furry friend blessed you?

_____

_____

_____

_____

_____

_____

_____

_____

_____

Your Personal Prayer:

_____

_____

_____

_____

_____

20

SISTERHOOD

What is sisterhood? Growing up with three brothers, I have often asked this question. There have been times I longed for a sister, like when my mother died, and I did not have a sister to reminisce memories with or mourn with—or during those difficult, adolescent, growing up moments when everyone is searching for identity, or after a breakup that left me heartbroken, the birth of my children, a disagreement with a best friend, or my frustration at a job—if only I had a sister I could really share my heart with.

Growing up, I had watched friends interacting with their sisters. It seemed when all else failed, meaning, when other people and friends let them down, they always had their sisters. Something told me that as sisters, they held each other's deepest secrets, good and bad, and no matter what, there was an untold loyalty. There was an agreement that all secrets were safe and sacred—that they always had each other's back. I saw my friends argue with their sisters, talk behind their backs, and even have cat fights where they wrestled each other to the ground, scratching and screaming at one another while still remaining best friends. Now if my friend and I got in a tussle like that, I guarantee we would not be best friends anymore!

What is it that sisters share that makes their relationship bond so loyal, faithful and forgiving? I would say it is because they are family. However, even family members often do not have such loyalty, love and forgiveness towards one another.

Having forged many women friendships over the years, I kind of have a clue about this. There are few friends I refer to as "sisters." And there were many who I thought were sisters, but I had to let go of them because their loyalty was broken. Believing the best in each other was no longer a part of the friendship.

I believe sisterhood is a sacred thing. It is an acceptance of one another, despite our faults, quirks, idiosyncrasies and differences. Sisterhood involves embracing each other just as we are. It means empowering one another with our successes and failures. It means mourning with each other during our losses.

Growing with each other as we maneuver our way through the journey of life is, perhaps, the real test of sisterhood. As we grow, our beliefs and ideologies about life may change and differ from one another. This can be threatening to our sister relationships. It makes us question our beliefs, and we wonder if we will still be accepted, rejected or judged because we seemingly think our sister has changed. I have lost several friendships this way that had a long history.

Honestly, it seemed as damning as a divorce. The rejection was grievous, and the judgment of ending the sister friendship left me feeling depressed, shameful and disoriented. I thought we were friends for life.

Intimate moments of sharing authentic conversations turned to gossip behind my back and mean conversations to my face. The sisterhood bond was broken and left me wondering if there ever was one.

What I have learned through the grievous times of sisterhood friendships ending out of rejection is the authenticity and value of true sisterhood. The ability to let go and grow is a forgiving process—the realization that I must be true to myself, even if it means letting go of a history of sisterhood friendship.

Sisterhood is a special bond. Oh, how we rejoice when we witness our daughter find that special friend she can relate to, have fun with and share special moments with. How wonderful it is when we see our mom having fun and belly-laughing with that lifelong friend whom she considers her sister.

There is such power in sister relationships. We learn from each other to have courage and love, forgiveness and empathy. We challenge each other to reach our goals and strive for the more that life has to offer. As sisters, we accept each other in the midst of our weaknesses and flaws, and therein, lies the power of sisterhood—the true magic of bonding as sisters. In all our weaknesses, losses and strengths, we accept each other with unconditional love, understanding and loyalty.

*Sweet friendships refresh the soul and awaken our hearts
with joy, for good friends are like the anointing oil that yields
the fragrant incense of God's presence.*

—Proverbs 27:9, TPT

Dear Lord,

*Thank You for the sisters You have brought into my life. Each one
has taught me so much. I am thankful for their love, kindness,
courage, faith and authenticity. They are a treasure to me and such a
gift from You. You heard my prayer of wanting a sister many years
ago as a young girl. You fulfilled my heart's desire, and I am thankful.*

Amen.

JOURNAL — Twenty

<u>Your Personal Journal:</u>

Friendships with sisterly bonds are a treasure.

Who are the sister friends in your life that are true and loyal?

How do you show your love and care to them?

_____

_____

_____

_____

_____

_____

_____

_____

_____

_____

<u>Your Personal Prayer:</u>

_____

_____

_____

_____

_____

21

THE TREASURE

gh drifts.
rted my walk. I'll nev
life or an hour or so of
classroom. I've walked
e the race-walkers behi
cond-winds and arm swin
nd mental health grow

*A*s I opened the large, beautifully framed doors to the library, I was struck with glee. I bounded to my prized possessions. I had waited all week for this adventure. As a young girl just learning how to read, it had become the highlight of my week. Every Friday night after supper, my Dad would take my brothers and I to the town library.

It was a majestic building with large cement steps and two huge pillars at the entrance way. There were two stone lions at the

The Treasure | 123

side of the steps to greet us. The dramatic entrance made it all the more enticing to me, as did the great adventure that awaited me there. My wandering eyes saw so many books to choose from.

As my Dad made his way to the grown up side of the library, I would venture off to the children's side. I would walk up and down each and every aisle noisily making discoveries of books I wanted to take home for the week.

I loved going to the library. I loved the smell of the books. I loved the freedom to roam around each aisle, looking for the animal books, the flower books, the story books that told of adventurous travels. I enjoyed "the people books," as I referred to them at my young age, which of course, were the biographies. The library was a treasure to me, a world of its own. Each Friday night I would get to discover this world.

My Dad was a lover of books. I would watch him devour books, magazines, and numerous newspaper articles each night after his work day. When we weren't going to the library to get books, we would receive numerous magazines in the mail; National Geographic, Reader's Digest, Time, Look, Life, and American Girl for me. These are only some of the ones that I recall as there were numerous others. We counted them as gifts in the mail, and it was so exciting to receive them.

I remember my father excitedly telling us how he was taking a speed reading class. I could see the elation all over his face as he told us he could read 700 words per minute.

After undergoing bypass surgery, my Dad made a habit of walking every night. He had a map taped to the door in the kitchen and made a commitment to himself to walk every street in town. He would then highlight on the map the street he walked. It was on these walks that he spoke into a small

124 | PATHWAYS TO PEACE

recorder. He would express his thoughts and impressions of what he saw and heard on his walk that day.

When he arrived home, he would begin typing his reflections in a journal. I fondly remember him getting the large, hard-cover Webster's Dictionary from the shelf each night. He would place this on the kitchen table where he set up his office, for easy access to find just the right word to express his deepest and sometimes whimsical thoughts to write in his journal.

I am not sure what my Dad enjoyed more, his beloved walks or his journaling. I do know that both gave him much happiness. Both gave him an appreciation for life with the love to freely express himself in his writing. He loved the discovery of finding new words and would circle them throughout his Webster's Dictionary. He prided himself on using them in his stories in his many journals.

When he passed, he left the journals in several manila envelopes. Opening each manila envelope, I felt as if I was opening something very sacred. I was. These were my father's journals, the journals of over 800 pages of his introspective thoughts.

The very words I heard him typing over the many years, I was now reading. It included the names of every street he walked at least a dozen times over, some I recognized, others I did not. The love that my father had for reading and writing were pouring out of these pages into my heart. It was then I realized the treasure my father had left me.

Webster's definition of "treasure":

1. a (1): wealth (such as money, jewels or precious metals) stored up or hoarded
        (2): wealth of any kind or in any form: RICHES

b   :a store of money in reserve
2.   : something of great worth or value
3.   : a collection of precious things

My father had stored up treasures for me all those Friday nights at the library—all those subscription magazines I received in the mail and all those nights I saw my dad with a book in hand—those were my treasures. The many times I heard "plunk, plunk, plunk" on his typewriter—those also were to be my treasures. He had placed treasures in my heart that would only grow more precious and valuable with time. Jewels, money and precious metals may lose their value over time, but this treasure of love my father had given me, with the treasure of reading and writing, will last forever.

Look with wonder at the depth of the Father's marvelous love that he has lavished on us! He has called us and made us his very own beloved children.

—1 John 3:1, TPT

∼

Father,

Thank You, for such a gift and treasure of a father's love that does not tarnish in time but remains as an everlasting treasure.

Amen.

JOURNAL — Twenty-One

<u>Your Personal Journal:</u>

Write your thoughts about the Treasure.

What people or places are the treasures in your heart?

What influence have they had in your life?

_____

_____

_____

_____

_____

_____

_____

_____

_____

_____

<u>Your Personal Prayer:</u>

_____

_____

_____

_____

_____

22

THE DAY I LOST MY BEST FRIEND

*E*verybody needs a best friend—that person to confide in, the one to whom you tell your deepest, darkest secrets, that one who makes you laugh (so hard you find yourself snorting with laughter!), someone who is there for you through thick and thin. That best friend for me has always been my mother. From the time I was a little girl, we were hitched at the hip.

The Day I Lost My Best Friend | 129

Every year we would watch the Wizard of Oz and all the Shirley Temple movies. We would share the laughter and tears of bonding together with these classics. The emotions of laughing and crying together that these movies tugged at your heart with, my mom and I shared. We embraced each other with love, fun and intimate moments—from sharing makeup tips, to praying prayers together, to exchanging recipes and cooking tips.

As a teen, facing an identity crisis and loneliness, Mom was there for me. Unconditional love was her strength to guide me and give me courage. During the dark times of my teenage years, trying to navigate through life, my mother's emotional support and unrelenting love gave me hope. Her bright smile and kind words told me, "It won't always be this way."

When I found the love of my life in my twenties, she rejoiced with me with extravagant joy. As I planned my wedding, she would share my giddiness and tolerate my impatience with the details. She was wise to give me advice and slow to get angry with my indecisiveness.

My Mom was a treasure of a best friend. We believed in each other. I would wipe her tears, and she would wipe mine, with no shame, just love. There was a gift of empowerment in our relationship. This empowerment that we shared gave us hope, courage, faith and a deep love and respect for each other, rejoicing with each other's wins and comforting one another during difficult times.

During one particular time during my tumultuous teenage years, I was angry at the world. Confused and distraught, I was in my bed room sobbing, feeling so lonely. Mom gently knocked on my door, and before I could yell, "Leave me alone!" she opened the door.

She sat next to me on my bed and lovingly stroked my hair, wiped my tears and calmly told me everything would be okay. She reassured me that I was loved and beautiful. Even though she did not have all the answers, or know the right thing to say, she told me she was there for me and would always be there for me. She told me she was my forever friend.

I did not realize then that one day I would be telling her the same thing. As Mom sat on her bed in the nursing home, looking disheveled and confused, angry and distraught, she told me she did not understand why she was there. Tears streamed down her face as she looked at me, desperate for answers.

Mom had been diagnosed with the beginning stages of dementia. I noticed changes over the past year in her personality, character and cheerful disposition. This once fun loving, compassionate, highly energetic Mom of mine was becoming impatient, intolerant, angry and increasingly depressed. I began noticing her forgetfulness and moments of confusion more and more.

She had just recently fallen and placed in a rehabilitation nursing home where she could heal and get some of her strength back, as she had not been eating well either.

My heart ached for her.

There is nothing worse than when you feel helpless to help your best friend, that one who's always been there for you, cheering you on, giving you loving advice and comforting you during life's messy moments. Oh, how I wanted so badly to fix this for her! To take all the confusion away, heal her body and bring joy and gladness to her heart and soul again.

I was brought back to my teenage days, many years ago, of that memory where my mother spoke her gentle loving words to me. When she told me that she did not have all the answers, or know all the right things to say. She told me how I was loved very much and that I was beautiful. She told me she would always be there for me and that she was my forever friend.

It was then that I wiped Mom's tear streaked face and held her in my hands. I told her how beautiful she was and how much I loved her. I told her that I did not have all the answers and didn't know all the right things to say, but what I did know was this: I would always be there for her, and I was her forever friend.

As she laid her head on my shoulder, we once again shared something very familiar to both of us, the comfort and love of a best friend. Everybody needs a best friend.

The day I lost my best friend happened over a period of time with this thing called dementia. It is ugly, damning and hurtful, ravaging the mind and body. So much of the person seems to be lost with this debilitating disease. However, one thing that can never be lost is the truth of love. This is the truth that best friends share, and this is the truth my mom and I shared.

I will never leave thee, nor forsake thee.

—Hebrews 13:5, KJV

He always comes alongside us to comfort us in every suffering so that we can come alongside those who are in any painful trial. We can bring them this same comfort that God has poured out upon us.

—2 Corinthians 1:4, TPT

132 | PATHWAYS TO PEACE

Dear Lord,

Help all those grieving with loved ones who are in this battle of dementia. Give grace and courage, faith and hope, especially on those dark daunting days. Let Your love be the power to see them through.

Amen.

JOURNAL — Twenty-Two

Your Personal Journal:

Do you have loved ones in your life dealing with dementia or disease?

What are some loving and gentle ways to interact with them?

_____

_____

_____

_____

_____

_____

_____

_____

_____

_____

Your Personal Prayer :

_____

_____

_____

_____

23

LETTING GO

*I*sn't it funny how life is all about letting go? I was 5 years old when I had my first encounter of letting go. My best friend moved miles away from me, and I just knew I would never see her again. We would never play Barbies together again, never eat chicken and dumplings together again, never chase her dog in the yard again, never giggle and giggle and roll on the floor laughing again. Our friendship was over.

Letting Go | 135

I still remember the day she said goodbye with her family all packed up in their 1962 station wagon. To make matters worse, it was a dreary rainy day with torrential downpours. It matched the matters of our hearts and the tears pouring down our little faces. I never felt such pain of letting go before. I felt the ache in my heart and the fear of never seeing my beloved friend again. I was losing my best friend and my heart felt broken.

Since that time, I have had to let go of many best friends. There was my hamster Josie, two little turtles that I got from my Nana's lake, two family dogs, my first grade teacher, my mother, my father, my grandmother and beloved aunts and uncles. I've had to release my three children into adulthood. Ready or not, they had to go.

I'm not sure if they were quite ready, but I knew that I wasn't. I understood that in order for them to grow and become adults, I had to let go. Even though I really didn't want to, I knew it had to be. I felt that familiar pain and ache in my heart once again.

Letting go is never easy. Whether it be our children, our parents, a best friend or a beloved pet, letting go is painful and can be heart wrenching. Sometimes letting go is an act of us walking away from a situation or an individual. Many times, letting go is where we have no choice on our part. It can be excruciating. Our heart feels torn. We may even feel alone and forsaken, fearful and scared.

A piece of our heart feels ripped out and we think, "Will this ache ever go away? This is so painful. I hate this!" There is grief in letting go; it hurts. To have something we've held close for so long and treasured so much, now gone—hurts. It simply hurts. Letting go is difficult, and the grief in letting go is real. It is a process to release the grief of letting go.

Oftentimes, there is anger, depression or loneliness that has to be worked through. Once we come to terms with these emotions and recognize them for what they are, our heart begins to heal. Reconstruction begins to take place, and hope returns. Letting go makes room in our heart for other things: new adventures, new friendships and growth in all areas of our life.

> *Trust in the Lord completely,*
> *and do not rely on your own opinions.*
> *With all your heart rely on him to guide you,*
> *and he will lead you in every decision you make.*
>
> —Proverbs 3:5, TPT

Dear Lord,

Give me grace to let go. Heal those places where I hurt and ache. Take my pain and grief and replace it with Your hope, healing and joy. Thank You for taking my hand as I let go and trust You to move me forward in all that You have for me.

Amen.

JOURNAL — Twenty-Three

<u>Your Personal Journal:</u>

Letting go can evoke feelings of fear and sadness.

Have there been times in your life where you had to let go?

What helped you let go and come to a place of peace?

_____

_____

_____

_____

_____

_____

_____

_____

_____

_____

<u>Your Personal Prayer About Letting Go:</u>

_____

_____

_____

_____

_____

24

ANTENNAS

*E*motions can be a very complicated thing. They can allow us to grow, or they can stifle our growth. We can bloom and become, or we can shut down and withdraw. In this cycle of life, I believe God desires that we learn to grow in our emotions and become all that we are meant to become. Emotions are antennas that navigate what we are experiencing in the stories of our life. Life is filled with emotions—celebrating a birth, mourning a death, experiencing the confusion of a betrayal, or rejoicing in a victory.

Antennas | 139

Life's emotions are both good and bad, ugly and sad, happy and joyful. To recognize and care for these emotions is key to a healthy, well-adjusted personhood. Many of our emotions come from the behaviors we learned during the years we grew up as children. We watch and learn from the adults around us how they react to different situations in life. We learn to mimic their responses, whether healthy or unhealthy, because this is the example we've been given. In doing so, we may not be able to recognize unhealthy emotions, or we feel unable to have control of them.

My dad was one who had a pretty stoic nature. He mostly kept his emotions to himself. He would laugh loudly, yell loudly, and talk excitedly. Yet, he held his sentimental emotions close to his chest, not ever really revealing them.

My Mom, on the other hand, basically wore her emotions on her sleeve. I knew if she was glad, sad or mad. There was no guesswork, and she was free to express that. Growing up into my own emotions, I was somewhat confused. When I found myself feeling sad, I'd have to ask myself, "I think I'm feeling sad; what am I feeling sad about?"

I'd get some introspection going on, replaying parts of my day and interaction with people. "Oh yes, what that person said hurt my feelings and that is why I must be feeling a little sad." You see, my dad's stoicism might have worked well for him, but not for me. That wasn't who I was.

I wasn't like my mother emotionally, either. I was me. I had to learn to control my emotions and practice some self-discipline. My emotions did not have free reign over me, tossing me around in every direction like the wind. I could discipline them and yet, at the same time, not stuff them down.

140 | PATHWAYS TO PEACE

I was becoming aware that growing up in my emotions not only took self-discovery, but self-discipline. To ignore our emotions, stunts our growth as a person and hinders our well-being. To have no control over them, also hinders our growth and full development as a healthy individual.

Upon returning home from school one day, I found my mom sitting at the kitchen table with a Kleenex in her hand, sobbing. She explained to me through her sobs that she just got the news that my young cousin of eighteen years old had just been killed in the Vietnam War. This was her sister's son.

Flashbacks of my cousin at my Gramma's house began running across my mind. On Sundays, all the aunts, uncles and cousins gathered at Gramma's. Those memories began flashing through my thoughts.

As my mom sobbed, I reached for another Kleenex for her and grabbed one for myself as well. I hurt for her and my aunt, uncle and cousin. My dad had left work early upon hearing the news and would be home shortly. I waited with Mom at the table, holding her hand as we comforted each other. I heard my dad's car enter the garage and as he opened the kitchen door, my mom ran into his arms crying of the tragic loss our family now faced.

I had never seen my dad cry before. This stoic man, my father, his eyes now filled with tears, holding my mom tightly, let me know that day that it is okay to grieve, cry and mourn.

Allowing our emotions freedom with care and discipline is an OKAY thing to do. My parents weren't always perfect in their emotions, but who is, really? My father, so stoic, holding back many times emotionally, and my Mom not holding back enough sometimes, has caused me to navigate myself emotion-

Antennas | 141

ally through life's ups and downs. I haven't done it all correctly either.

Many times, I had grace. Other times, not so much. However, I'm learning that when I take care of my emotions, it is for the betterment of myself and those around me, just as it is with our health and physical well-being (and anything else in our life for that matter). Emotional healing, development and well-being happen over a period of time. It takes recognizing our emotions, being honest with them and not suffocating them but nurturing them to be healthy.

Emotions are antennas that navigate what we are experiencing in the stories of our life. Perhaps you have had emotional trauma or not very good examples of emotional well-being in your life. It is never too late to be made well emotionally. Pray with me.

Looking unto Jesus the author and perfecter of our faith,

—Hebrews 12:2, ASV

～

Dear Lord,

You are the Author and Giver of life. You desire for me to have good, healthy emotions. Heal me emotionally where I need healing. Set me free to respond to life healthily and to be wise in my emotions. Bless me emotionally, to hear and see clearly and to respond accordingly.

Thank You, Giver of emotions, that we can enjoy this precious gift called life.

Amen.

JOURNAL — Twenty-Four

<u>Your Personal Journal:</u>

Emotions are tricky. They have a way of sneaking up on us. It's important to understand them and to navigate our way through life with them in order to have peace. God is not the author of confusion, but of peace.

Have your emotions ever caused havoc on you?

In what ways can you pursue peace so they do not rule over you?

_____

_____

_____

_____

_____

_____

_____

_____

<u>Your Personal Prayer:</u>

_____

_____

_____

_____

_____

25

THE BULLY & ARBOR DAY

I had just received my paper back after my 4th grade teacher slapped it on my desk. It wasn't my best grade, but it wasn't my worst either. It was not a secret that I didn't excel in math. I hated math, and my classmate sitting next to me knew it.

He loved math and aced every assignment. When we aced an assignment in that classroom, the teacher put a big gold seal on the top of the paper. My classmate next to me always received

The Bully & Arbor Day | 145

big gold seals, not only on his math papers, but every paper he completed. He received one big gold seal after another. He would proudly place his gold seal paper on the top left hand corner of his desk, on my side of course, and make sure I would see it every single time. Of course he was proud. Who wouldn't be?

He was known as the "Brainiac" of the classroom. And of course, he had to be sitting next to me. I was a good student but not a gold seal on every paper type of student. Sometimes, when he would get his paper and I would get mine, he would hold it up in front of my face and give me a disapproving smirk. I anticipated this every day: the smirk, the gold seal, and the disapproval.

It started to play havoc on my self-esteem, especially the math papers. Mine were usually failing, and his were always gold seals. The teacher wasn't too pleased with my constant failing math papers, but it seemed like she danced as she handed him his gold star math papers. I was beginning to feel bullied as he grimaced, laughing under his breath, as he got a gold star paper. I was slithering with humiliation and defeat. I wanted a gold seal so bad.

One day my teacher went to the front of the classroom and told us there was an exciting contest that was going to take place in the school. She told us about a special day called, "Arbor Day." It was a day recognized as a holiday celebrating trees.

I had always been a plant lover, even as a little girl I had a table in my bedroom lined with plants. I had named each one; yes, I named them! Each leaf and texture I found so interesting. I knew which one to water and when. I knew exactly which one needed more sunlight than the other and my plants thrived. Now my teacher had my attention.

146 | PATHWAYS TO PEACE

She explained that each student was to write a story about Arbor Day and the planting of trees. There would be three winners from the entire school. The students that won would get to plant a tree with the principal in the front school yard. I was so excited about this.

I was already beginning to form the story in my mind. When school dismissed, I ran home, went immediately to my room and began working on my story. It was about a little girl who longed to plant a tree on Arbor Day. I don't remember all the facts, or the entire storyline, but I do remember how giddy and excited I was to write the story of this little girl planting a tree on Arbor Day! I can still see myself sitting at the desk in my bedroom, smiling, happily writing the story with hopeful expectancy of planting that tree with my school principal.

The day came to turn in my paper. My classmate looked at me ever so smugly as he pridefully handed his paper into the teacher. I smiled with high hopes as I handed her mine.

Finally, the day came when the teacher was going to announce the winners and hand out the gold seal papers. I felt that butterfly feeling in my stomach as she walked towards me and my classmate sitting next to me, the gold star champion. My heart was beating fast as I anticipated who that gold star paper was going to go to.

She then turned to me with a big smile and said "Congratulations! You are the gold star winner and will plant the tree with the principal!" The whole class applauded as joy danced through my entire being! I don't think I could've smiled any bigger. I was so excited and happy. My classmate friend gave me a dirty look and winced as I placed my gold star paper in the corner of my desk for him to see.

The following day the other contestant winners and I went with the principal to plant our trees in the front school yard as the entire school body watched with pride. It was a special day, this Arbor Day, one I will never forget.

The sun was so bright and pretty and the sky was a beautiful blue. As I picked up my shovel and placed it in the ground, I felt such a feeling of satisfaction, pride and so much joy that I could participate in this moment of planting such a beautiful tree. It would grow tall and lovely, spreading its roots and giving off shade from its luscious green leaves.

From then on, my classmate wasn't such a show-off bully anymore. My teacher seemed less angry with my math scores. My heart was enlarged with purpose and fulfillment. I was learning more about myself and my abilities, rather than my disabilities. Every time I arrived at school in the morning and left school at the end of day, I had to pass that little tree I planted. It, too, reminded me of my abilities, achievements and creativity.

Every believer has received grace gifts, so use them to serve one another as faithful stewards of the many-colored tapestry of God's grace.

—1 Peter 4:10, TPT

∼

Dear Lord,

Thank You for the abilities and gifts You place in each one of us. Each one of us is so unique and special from the other. No two are the

148 | PATHWAYS TO PEACE

same, for we are fearfully and wonderfully made. It is with love and joy You create each one of us. May we use these gifts and abilities for Your good pleasure.

Amen.

JOURNAL — Twenty-Five

<u>Your Personal Journal:</u>

It's important to acknowledge and steward the gifts that God has given to each one of us.

List 3 attributes and talents you have.

In what ways can you enrich them?

_____

_____

_____

_____

_____

_____

_____

_____

_____

_____

<u>Your Personal Prayer:</u>

_____

_____

_____

_____

26

THE RIPTIDES OF LIFE

We had come to the beach that day, longing for the fresh ocean air and the cool, brisk waters of the Atlantic coast. After a long Connecticut winter, we were anticipating the warm sunshine, beach sand and riding waves.

We tried to make several trips to the coast every summer before the season changed to cold weather again. I had come here often as a little girl and was enjoying it with my husband and family.

As we unloaded the car with our beach blankets, umbrellas, and a cooler full of snacks and drinks, we could hear the waves slamming into the shore. As we climbed over the dunes we could see the waves, almost viciously, crashing into the coastland. My son and his friend excitedly ran into the water as my husband dove in after them. At fifteen years old, full of adventure and zeal, there was no holding my son and his friend back. My husband always enjoyed the ocean, swimming and riding the waves. I enjoyed riding the waves, too. It was the highlight of going to the beach each summer.

That day I stayed with my 18 month old daughter on shore, playing with sand buckets and making sand castles together. Instead of riding the waves, I was too busy chasing my daughter to and fro as she chased the waves, rolling in and out.

As I looked out to the crashing waves and roaring ocean, I couldn't help but notice that the waves were getting quite high. They seemed violent at times, to the point where I was getting concerned. I heard someone else close by mention that a storm was rolling in and there were notices to be careful and cautious.

By this time, my husband and my son, along with his friend, were out quite a distance. Trying to keep an eye on them and my busy daughter, who wanted to discover her surroundings, was becoming a challenge for me. I then noticed my son waving his hand and yelling.

At first I thought he was yelling; "Hey! Hi mom!" And then quickly, as he drifted further and further away, I realized he was yelling for help! I looked for my husband and noticed he was within feet of him, but didn't seem to be going anywhere.

"Why isn't he moving faster? Does he know my son is yelling for help? Move! Move!" I yelled!

152 | PATHWAYS TO PEACE

It then occurred to me that my husband was struggling like my son and he, too, could not move. My son's friend seemed to be moving further out, also. Now they were getting further and further away from each other, and further and further away from me. They were beginning to look like dots out in the ocean.

Panic set in. I knew there was not much time as I realized a riptide was carrying them away. I wanted to run out and save them. It was my first reaction, yet I knew I was not able to do so. My daughter began running in another direction as I struggled to focus where they were. I frantically looked around for a life-guard, but I did not see one close by.

I then began yelling: "Somebody help them! They need help! Somebody please go to them and help them!" As I cried out frantically and desperately, praying a thousand prayers, some teenage boys, who were in the water, heard my cry and their cries for help also.

Without hesitation, these young men swam feverishly out to where they were, as a lifeguard or two also joined them. I watched panic stricken as they gathered my husband, my son and his friend trying to draw them back inland.

Just as they started making their way back, I could see several more ferocious waves making their way towards them. Strong, mighty waves knocked each one of them under the water as I waited with terror for them to come back up.

Ferocious waters dragged them out one more time before they could get their balance and strength to make their way back to land again. It was a terrifying struggle, as each of them fought their way back. They returned and landed flat on their backs, completely out of breath and strength.

The Riptides of Life | 153

Tears, exhaustion and fatigue consumed them as we held each other tight and tighter still. It was one of the most frightening events in our lives that each of us had ever faced.

I am so grateful for the brave, teenage young men and the lifeguards who heard our cries for help. I am so grateful that they didn't hesitate to help them when they swam with vigor to rescue them. The soberness of that day stayed with us for many days.

Still, to this day, we are mindful and cautious of dangerous tides of the waters. Many times you don't know where the riptide is, and you suddenly find yourself caught in it as it drags you out to dangerous waters, deeper and deeper.

Life has many twists and turns where, oftentimes, we don't realize the sinking waters until we are in them. Many times they take us by surprise: job losses, sicknesses, diseases or unexpected situations that test the very core of our being and personhood.

We feel desperate and scared, fighting to survive the treacherousness of what is pulling us under. We find ourselves losing the footing of solid ground, crying out for help and a place of safety, once again.

I cannot imagine what that day would have held if it were not for the helpers, the life givers. They saved my husband's and son's lives, and that of his friend. During times of crisis in our life, we need helpers.

We need the life givers: those who offer strength, courage and empathy in our time of need. Life can be like crashing waves and riptides taking us further out from our place of safety. It is then we need helpers to hear our cries for help. The helpers are the ones to lead us to a place back to safety and peace.

154 | PATHWAYS TO PEACE

I want to be a helper—one who leads the hurting back to a safe place, one who has courage and empathy to help, heal and restore.

I will never forget the danger of that day. I will never forget the riptide of the tumultuous waters that day. I will never forget the prayers I prayed in those moments of desperation. I will always remember the helpers of that day.

In the riptide moments of life, may we be the helpers, the givers of safety and peace to those in need.

God is our refuge and strength, a very present help in trouble.

—Psalms 46:1, KJV

Dear Lord,

You are the Sovereign Helper in the riptide moments of our life. You are the One who rescues, restores and brings us to a place of peace and safety. May we also help those around us to a place of safety and peace in the riptide moments of life.

Thank You for the courage and strength to be those helpers.

Amen.

JOURNAL — Twenty-Six

Your Personal Journal:

At times, life can be like crashing waves with riptides taking us further out from our place of safety. These are times in our life where we may need helpers and peacemakers.

Who are the helpers and peacemakers in your life during difficult times?

_____

_____

_____

_____

_____

_____

_____

_____

Your Personal Prayer:

_____

_____

_____

_____

_____

27

NO FEAR

I hate fear. It is the most uncomfortable feeling in the world. It is one of those emotions you feel you have no control over. I have felt fear many times in my life—a fear of losing someone I love, a fear of disease, a fear of moving, a fear of growing old, a fear of change. You name it, there are so many things that one can be afraid of.

Life has fear, and I do not believe anyone that tells me they have no fear. Each one of us has faced this Goliath at one time or another—perhaps many times, because to live this life, there will be fear. It is an emotion just like many other emotions we experience during our lifetime.

The positive emotions of love, joy and peace we grasp. We accept them with open arms and an open heart.

We often find ourselves doing the same thing with fear. We receive its lies and taunts of accusation. We follow it into a dark cave, only looking for a way of escape. Fear is a dreaded thing.

I don't know anyone who likes fear. It comes in different shapes and sizes. It makes its way like a slithering snake, disguising itself through people, circumstances and dilemmas. Its voice lies to us, telling us there is no way out. Fear often comes with a trace of truth and exaggerates itself into a full blown lie.

When I was pregnant with my first child at the sweet age of 23, ultrasounds were not given. Even though I read an entire library of all the pregnancy books I could get my hands on, I still wanted the security and confirmation that the little one in my pouch was doing just fine.

Fear would talk to me sometimes to suggest things were not fine. How I wished I could peek inside for just a moment to see for myself that my little person was doing just fine, happily sucking his thumb. Born 7lbs. 7 oz., he was more than fine.

Fear gripped me as I witnessed both of my parents being treated for cancer. The fear of helplessness and grief of losing them terrorized me at times. Grace was my friend who gave me courage and strength.

Fear has no mercy. It doesn't compromise with our sad or desperate feelings. It ridicules, taunts and insults. It is a mean, harassing thing that tries to dismantle our faith, hope and love.

158 | PATHWAYS TO PEACE

My muscles have grown stronger facing this giant of fear. I've had to exercise them in order to make them tougher to defeat fear's lies and tactics. Fear doesn't like to give up easily. It sends in its accompanying comrades of worry and anxiety. To overcome fear, one cannot compromise their position of defense. You must have a shield of faith which gives you hope.

Hope believes that no matter the circumstance or situation, there is always hope ahead. Hope for wellness. Hope for healing. Hope for restoration. Turn your heart towards hope in times of fear.

Fear likes us to believe that it has all the power. It does not. We have the power to accept it or reject it. We must reject fear at all cost because to receive it only weakens us.

It weakens our faith, hope and love. The power lies in rejecting or accepting fear's lies, taunts and accusations. Fear comes from a dark place. It does not come from God, the Giver of life.

God is a God of love, light and truth. As I draw near to God in times of harassing fear, the light of love is drawn in, and I receive truth. Truth sets me free from fear. All its destructive ways find themselves diminishing and laid to rest.

Love lights the way. There is no fear in love. The more I allow the love and the truth of God's love into my life, the freer I become. Fear cannot touch me there, though it tries. It cannot live there.

God's love is faithful to heal and restore all the places that fear tried to rob. Fear has no place where God's love abides. Nothing can separate us from the love of God, not even fear.

There is no fear in God's love, only perfect peace.

For God will never give you the spirit of fear, but the Holy Spirit who gives you mighty power, love, and self-control.

—2 Timothy 1:7, TPT

Dear God,

Thank You for Your all-consuming love that guards and protects us, even in times of fear. In Your love is light, truth and peace.

Amen.

JOURNAL — Twenty-Seven

Your Personal Journal:

We have the power to accept or reject fear. There is no fear in God's love, only perfect peace.

In what ways have you overcome fear?

_____

_____

_____

_____

_____

_____

_____

_____

_____

Your Personal Prayer:

_____

_____

_____

_____

_____

28

"MOM, BREATHE! I'M OKAY!"
MOTHER'S DAY

      Being a mother is one of the greatest gifts I have received in my life. It is also one of the most challenging and frightening responsibilities I have ever been given. My responsibility to nurture, raise, guide and protect these three incredible, fascinating individuals to the best of my ability is not only a daunting and extraordinary responsibility and gift, it is an honor in the highest regard.

"Mom, Breathe! I'm OKAY!" | 163

I love being a mother. It has brought me to blood, sweat and tears numerous times over. This motherhood gig has caused me to do things I thought were impossible. Has it always been pie in the sky easy? No. Has it played out as romantic as those sweet TV commercials with a mother and child laughing, holding hands as they run through a field of flowers? Not always. Has it stretched me in ways and places I didn't even know existed within myself? Yes.

I have seen enough broken bones, pus and blood to make Rambo squirm. I love being a mother and that is why this year, for Mother's Day, I am asking for more.

It all began for me at the tender age of 23, giving birth to my first child. My husband and I had taken weeks of childbirth classes where I was given techniques on how to breathe.

These certain breathing exercises and techniques would help me during times of contractions and pushing. It all seemed so easy at the time. The instructions were sensible and clear, and my breathing exercises seemed to produce good results.

Now here I lay with sweat dripping from every part of my body, capillaries bursting through my face and my husband annoyingly telling me to breathe. It was all so sweet when he was instructing me to breathe while in the childbirth classes. It all seemed so easy and quite perfect then.

I had decided not to take the epidural or even a Tylenol. It was 1981; *au naturel* was in, and I was determined to do this exactly that way. So, I breathed. Slowly breathe in, slowly exhale. Slowly breathe in, slowly exhale. You're doing fine, hubby lovingly tells me, you're doing fine. Just breathe.

And so, this happens to be the best advice I have learned as a mother. To breathe. Slowly and calmly, breathe.

164 | PATHWAYS TO PEACE

I found myself needing this advice once again when my daughter was two and decided to hide behind a tree in the woods behind our home. It seemed we were playing in the yard one minute, I turned around to look at a plant, and poof, she was gone! Just like that.

In the blink of an eye, my little two year old decided to happily run off to hide behind a tree.

Panic struck me as I frantically yelled out her name to no avail. I found myself running wildly around the yard in every direction, screaming like a mad woman until my voice grew hoarse. I could hardly breathe as I nervously and tearfully called 911. When the operator asked me to describe what she was wearing, I went blank. What kind of mother am I that I could not remember what my daughter was wearing?

Just as I was searching my brain to describe what my daughter was wearing, my neighbor yelled to me, "We found her!"

And there she was, hiding ever so innocently behind a tree, eating her lollipop. I cried and laughed at the same time as I scooped her up in my arms. Breathe, I told myself, just breathe!

It was half an hour past the time of my son's usual arrival home from his first job...and then, the phone call came.

"I've been in an accident, Mom...I'm OKAY. It's OKAY!"

I found myself yelling into the phone out of fright and worry: "Where are you? Where are you?" I quickly grabbed my purse and keys and rushed to the sight of fire trucks, policemen and my son laid out on a stretcher.

My knees cave and vomit rises in my throat. I think I am going to throw up. My son sees the look of horror on my face and tells me, "Mom, breathe! I'm OKAY!"

"Mom, Breathe! I'm OKAY!" | 165

"Well, I'm not!" I exclaim back to him, holding back the tears.

And so it is, from the time I find out I am pregnant with each of them—I learn to breathe. You'd think I'd have this motherhood thing down by now. New challenges arrive with each one. New love arrives with each one. New necessities arrive with each one.

This is why I am asking for more this Mother's Day. Not more flowers or more charm bracelets, and not even more fancy dinners. I find that no matter how many books I read on the art of mothering—from breastfeeding to college searching—it is not enough.

Nothing prepares us for the skin-scraping, heart-wrenching, soul-searching reality moments we will encounter with our children.

No matter what age or what season, we, as moms, will always need more. More wisdom. More love. More nourishment. More kindness. More patience. More groove. More knowledge. More confidence. More peace. More, more and more of all the things that will make a difference in their lives... and mine as well.

As I learn to breathe--and breathe again—my way through this gift of motherhood is to always ask for more. To Jay, Dan and Julia, my beloved children and gifts from God, I will always ask for more. I will not settle for less and I will always ask for more.

Her teachings are filled with wisdom and kindness as loving instruction pours from her lips."

—Proverbs 31:26, TPT

166 | PATHWAYS TO PEACE

Dear Father,

Thank You ever so much for this gift of motherhood. Thank You for these beautiful, wonderful children You have blessed me with. They are teaching me so much. As I learn to breathe with the loveliness of being their mother, You, dear Lord, are strong where I am weak. I will continue to ask for more of all I need to give to my children and all they may need to face the challenges and gift of life.

Amen.

JOURNAL — Twenty-Eight

<u>Your Personal Journal:</u>

As moms, we are continually evolving as our children continue to grow from babies to teens, to young adults and then to parents of their own. God is faithful to meet us where we are at in this gift of motherhood. We just have to remember to breathe.

_____

_____

_____

_____

_____

_____

_____

_____

<u>Your Personal Prayer:</u>

_____

_____

_____

_____

29

THE SUNFLOWER

*S*unflowers hold a special meaning to me. They are bright and beautiful, and you can't help but smile and feel light hearted when you see one. They also hold a special memory for me.

Every summer, my Dad would grow the largest and most massive sunflowers. By mid-July, they were towering toward the sky. At least, it seemed so to this little girl who had to stretch her neck way up to see them. They looked like a kingdom

The Sunflower | 169

flower to me—mighty and strong with such a majestic, yellow color as bright as the sun.

Each morning, I would walk outside and marvel at how much taller they seemed than the day before. I can still see the delight on my dad's face, smiling with pride at how beautifully and lovely the sunflowers were growing.

During the day, I would watch them grow and face the sun. It seemed as if they were smiling each time. As I peered through my bedroom window, I would play with the adventures dancing through my mind of climbing up the majestic sunflower to the sky. The towering sunflowers had reached my second story window where I could watch them gracefully sway in the wind as the giant, green leaves swayed with them.

To this day, I plant sunflowers along my fence because it warms my heart with good memories of my dad. It is my way of saying, "Hi Dad! Thank you for teaching me about sunflowers!"

What I especially love about them is, no matter how I plant them, they always turn to face the sun. That is what sunflowers do. I have learned many lessons from the sunflower. Although they are a hardy flower, they do appreciate the sturdiness of a fence. It is advisable to grow them along a fence to shelter them from the strong winds that can cause damage to the stems.

There are so many captivating truths about the sunflower to be learned and appreciated. They remind us to have a positive attitude and a sunny disposition, to spread seeds of happiness, to hold our heads high and to be strong and courageous.

The one that speaks louder than all the rest is how this majestic sunflower, with its deep roots and strong stems, does best when planted near a sturdy fence. It then has some form of protection from the strong winds when they do come.

170 | PATHWAYS TO PEACE

I have found that during the trying times, during the winds of adversity in life, when we are trying to face the sun, that leaning on a fence helps keep us steady and strong. It is during these times that I know my Heavenly Father is also looking over the fence of His promises at me. He meets me where I am. He delights in me as I grow and learn from the lessons in life. Smiling at me with pride, He looks over the fence to see how beautiful and lovely I am becoming in His eyes.

It is then that I look up and say, "Hi Dad! Thank You for being the keeper of my heart."

O God, how extravagant is your cherishing love! All mankind can find a hiding place under the shadow of your wings.

—Psalms 36:7, TPT

Dear Heavenly Father,

Thank You for all the times You looked after me over the fence of life, protecting me and shielding me from the storms and winds of life. Thank You for giving me sunshine and warmth to grow into my destiny, future and purpose.

A wonderful Dad You are.

Amen.

JOURNAL — Twenty-Nine

<u>Your Personal Journal:</u>

The sunflower is one of my all time favorite flowers. It is a healthy reminder to me to face the sun and see the good things in life.

In the garden of life, what is your favorite flower?

Does it hold a special memory or meaning to you?

_____

_____

_____

_____

_____

_____

_____

_____

<u>Your Personal Prayer:</u>

_____

_____

_____

_____

_____

30

TWO WORDS

I went to bed tossing and turning with a heavy heart. Another shooting had taken place, and I found myself mourning the loss of young lives, police officers and the mothers and fathers who lost their beloved children.

Distressed emotions ransacked me with the ongoing pains of the animosity of today's politics, media and news sites. My emotions were sad, angry and forlorn. I was feeling stuck with no answers of resolution for my peace.

Two Words | 173

I remember as a child, kneeling by my bed at night, thanking God for peace as I envisioned people all across the land holding hands in peace. With that, I would go to bed, smiling. Tonight was not one of those nights. Instead, I went to bed with a distraught heart, asking God for answers.

"Where is the peace? Why are we in such turmoil with one another?" Naive questions for a grown woman. As a grown woman though, I still want peace.

I believe we all want peace. Young and old, no matter our age or race, nation or tribe—we all want peace. I don't know how long it was or how many hours passed before I finally gave up my struggle of tossing and turning and finally fell asleep.

Upon waking, I still found myself asking questions to my distraught heart and to God. Questions of, "What can be done? What can be done? Where is the peace?" As I quieted myself in a moment of prayer, I heard two words.

"Show up."

"Show up" is what I heard. Two simple words: "Show up."

"Show up to what?" I asked.

- Show up and give the hurting compassion.
- Show up and listen to that elderly person tell that story one more time.
- Show up and listen to that young child tell their story.
- Show up and give that homeless person a bottle of water and a smile.
- Show up and call your mom.
- Show up and hug your dad.
- Show up and tell your kids you love them.
- Show up and buy groceries for someone.

174 | PATHWAYS TO PEACE

- Show up and smile at people today.
- Show up.
- Show up and be patient.
- Show up and be gentle.
- Show up and be loving.
- Show up and pray.
- Show up and be the light of peace.

As I saw the sun rise that morning, peeping through my bedroom window, it began to chase away the darkness. The light became brighter and brighter as it illuminated the darkness.

The answer to my questions were greeting me. "Show up," it simply said.

It became clear to me, and peace began to still my wandering mind and heart. To show up and give what we have—a smile, a kind heart, or a listening ear—brings light and love. In light and love, we have peace, a peace that passes understanding.

Today, I decided I am going to show up, and I hope that you will, too.

And everything I've taught you is so that the peace which is in me will be in you and will give you great confidence as you rest in me. For in this unbelieving world you will experience trouble and sorrows, but you must be courageous, for I have conquered the world!"

—John 16:33, TPT

∼

Two Words | 175

Dear Lord,

Give us the courage to show up. In the midst of feeling distraught, tired or weary, give us the strength to show up. Give us what we need to make this world a better place.

In a world in need of peace, allow us to show up with a peace that passes understanding—Your peace, the light and love of God.

Amen.

JOURNAL — Thirty

<u>Your Personal Journal:</u>

Often we find ourselves wanting to retreat when the world around us is facing difficult and troubling times. In cultivating and promoting peace, it is during these times we need to be the helpers, extending kindness and compassion.

What can you do to brighten someone's day?

Who is someone you can encourage today?

_____

_____

_____

_____

_____

_____

_____

_____

<u>Your Personal Prayer:</u>

_____

_____

_____

_____

31

DENISE'S WINDOW BOX

I began Denise's Window Box in 2012. I felt a nudge to begin a Facebook page where I could share things that inspired me. I had hoped to give others encouragement and some faith, hope and love along the way. I myself had just gone through some tumultuous times that tried my faith, dampened my hope and tested my love. I was getting encouragement on other pages on the internet, including those of home decor, uplifting faith, cooking and gardening. I found myself getting uplifted as I read the messages of faith and hope.

Denise's Window Box | 179

My creative juices were stirred up as I read gardening, crafting and recipe sites.

During a dark and isolated time in my life, I found these particular internet sites lifting my spirits and morale. I then started feeling a nudge to create my own site. At first, I immediately rejected the nudge and pushed the thought away.

"No way!" I told myself. First of all, I had no idea how to go about building a web page, let alone an audience. Secondly (the reason that was weighing on me the most), I felt I had nothing to give. I was trying to scrape *myself* off the floor—how could I give hope, healing and love to others (and strangers at that)?

However, each night as I went to bed, I was faced with the strong impression to create a page where people could receive faith, hope and love. My, "No way!" started to become a, "Maybe." I began considering what I could share to lighten the path of someone's life just a little bit more. I thought of the things I loved and the things and moments that brought joy to my life.

I have always loved flowers, plants and gardening. I love the beach—the water, seashells and everything that goes with that. I enjoy cooking and creating recipes. I adore my Melody, whom I call my angel kitty. I have fun making simple crafts from a dime with great satisfaction. I have surrounded myself with devotional and reflective books, and I am a daily reader of the Bible.

So, I saw that perhaps I did have some things I could share with others. As I was in the considering mode, which I kept to myself, pondering in my heart, the nudge grew stronger to where I finally took the plunge.

180 | PATHWAYS TO PEACE

Did I feel ready? No. Was I scared? Yes. What if nobody came to my page? What if I don't know how to do this at all? What if I'm laughed at? I still felt like I had nothing to give. There were many what-ifs along the way and many questions, too. I forged ahead anyway because the nudging was invading my privacy!

I began my first post with photos of lighthouses. I didn't write too much but just shared the inspiration and beauty of what they are and represent. Suddenly, one, two, then three responses. It was so exciting to get these first responses! That day, my page soon had 10 followers, growing up to 25. Within days, friends of the Window Box had grown to a few hundred. And now, several years later, it is well over 40,000!

What amazes me in all of this is that *in my times of weakness* I was nudged to give. I felt like I had nothing to give. I had been receiving hope, faith, encouragement and love along the way, and yet I still felt like I had nothing to give. However, a substance was growing inside of me, making itself ready to give to others.

I was reminded of the story in the Bible where a little boy gave Jesus his five small loaves of bread and two fishes to feed a crowd of five thousand (John 6:1-14). This is all he had. It did not look like enough to feed this crowd. It certainly was not enough to feed this size crowd. However, he gave Jesus all he had. Then Jesus used it for the good and multiplied it as well. In my weakness, I gave all that I had, which felt like very little. And yet, I saw God use it for good.

I have met people all over the world via the internet, forming a "pen pal" friendship, sharing faith, hope and love. In giving, I have received. My heart has been enriched and enlarged in so many ways I cannot even begin to describe. We have been with each other during joyous times, tragic times in our nation and in the daily walk of life. *Denise's Window Box* changed my life, all because I said "Yes" to a nudge that inspired me to give out of my weakness.

The greatest thing that I have learned is this: People everywhere—no matter their race, religion, gender, faith, or age—all want and need the same things: faith, hope, love, friendship, kindness, peace, a listening ear and encouragement along life's journey. I have received this more than I could ever hope for through my many friends at *Denise's Window Box*. What set out to be a gift for others, in turn, has been a gift to me.

Please join me at *Denise's Window Box* on Facebook.

> *Trust in the Lord with all thine heart; and lean not unto thine own understanding. In all thy ways acknowledge him, and he shall direct thy paths."*

—Proverbs 3:5-6, KJV

Dear Lord,

Thank You for Your nudges to lead us and guide us in this journey of life. In our weakness, You bring us out of hiding to make us strong. To give is to receive.

May Your light shine brighter and brighter within each one of us so that we can truly give to one another hope, faith, love and peace.

Amen.

JOURNAL — Thirty-One

Your Personal Journal:

Denise's Window Box changed my life. I have met so many wonderful people from all over the world sharing faith, hope and love. This led me to pursue my dreams and write this book.

What dreams are in your heart?

_____

_____

_____

_____

_____

_____

_____

_____

_____

Your Personal Prayer:

_____

_____

_____

_____

EPILOGUE

*P*eace is a gift you give yourself. Through this journey of life, I am learning that peace is not something tangible that you can grab onto. One cannot automatically have peace with money or fancy cars, beautiful homes or wealth. Position or status quo does not give one peace. It may, just for a moment in time. Just as in an ocean-view sunset or a quiet, serene nature walk, there's a sense of peace and resolve just for that moment in time.

True, valid, sincere inner-peace comes from within. It comes from coming to terms with the "not so nice" situations and difficulties in life. Inner-peace happens when we learn how to handle difficult life situations and people in our life. Well-founded and well-grounded peace takes place when we come to a place of forgiveness, forgiving the misfortunes in our life as well as the hurtful and difficult people in our life. At times, it even comes by forgiving ourselves from guilt, shame and remorse feelings.

Peace is an ongoing process because life is an ongoing process. It is a constant pathway to be walked. It is a journey of

Epilogue | 185

wonderful times, difficult times and sorrowful times as well. Peace teaches us how to navigate through them all. Peace comes to reside within us as we acknowledge our emotions and the truth with ourselves and our God. It is only when we do so that we will have that perfect peace that passes understanding.

Oftentimes, we need help with the transparency of being honest with ourselves and with God. I know I do. It is in these times that I go to God in prayer. I have found that there is no perfect way to pray. Whether it be a long prayer or a short prayer, it does not matter. It is all a matter of the heart to God and our heart yielded to His in honesty and transparency. In that, a pathway to peace is being formed. This pathway plows through the hurdles and obstacles of life, shining a light that will lead and guide us in times of storms and difficulty. Inner-peace comes to still our soul and comfort our heart. The gift of peace resides so that we may be peacemakers, peacekeepers and peace givers.

My hope is that as you read the stories, prayers and reflections in *Pathways to Peace*—while journaling your own reflections and prayers as well—that you, too, will journey on with the gift of peace on *your* pathway.

Love and Peace to you.

Sincerely,

Denise Allen

The Window Box

ABOUT THE AUTHOR

Denise Allen is a New England native, wife, and mother of three. She is the founder of *Denise's Window Box* on Facebook and the author of *the Window Box Series*. Her writings inspire people with faith, hope and love, guiding them to a place of peace. Denise's hobbies include gardening, bike riding, DIY projects and her sweet kitty, Melody.